A Work of
Beauty

A Work of Beauty

Alexander McCall Smith's Edinburgh

Published in 2014 by the
Royal Commission on the Ancient and
Historical Monuments of Scotland
(RCAHMS)

John Sinclair House, 16 Bernard Terrace
Edinburgh EH8 9NX

+44(0)131 662 1456
info@rcahms.gov.uk
www.rcahms.gov.uk

Registered Charity SC026749

British Library Cataloguing-in-Publication
Data. A catalogue record for this book is
available from the British Library.

ISBN 9781902419862

Designed by Oliver Brookes
Typeset in Garamond and Gill Sans
Printed in Poland by Perfekt

frontispiece
The east end of Princes Street, 2014
RCAHMS DP194949

Royal
Commission on the
Ancient and
Historical
Monuments of
Scotland

Contents

6   Preface

8   A Work of Beauty

54   City of Literature

82   Seat of Learning

120   Working Lives

164   Of Doctors and Scientists

192   City of the Mind

220   End Piece

222   Acknowledgements

223   Index

Preface

Who can resist an old photograph album? There is a particular pleasure in turning the pages of the record of a family's life. Here are the children on their first day back at school; here is an aunt on her bicycle; here is our first house; here is the dog thinking about what to do next. It does not really matter if you do not know the people in the photographs – anonymous photographs can be every bit as appealing, perhaps even more so, as those featuring people we know. The fascination often lies in the detail: the places in which the picture was taken, the clothes everybody was wearing, the make and model of car in the background.

In the collection of the Royal Commission on the Ancient and Historical Monuments of Scotland (RCAHMS) there are many hundreds of such photographic albums recording, in their very particular way, the life of the people of Scotland. Those albums make up just a tiny part of an astonishingly rich archive of photographs, drawings and maps that the Commission looks after. It is an important component of the nation's memory. This is the richest and best-preserved visual record of Scotland's human and natural terrain – its towns, its cities, its countryside. It includes not only very early photographs taken by pioneers of photography, but also aerial views taken by the latest technology; it contains architectural drawings for individual dwellings and plans for whole urban swathes. It records not only the public face of the country –

what we can all see when we walk along the street – but the things that are behind the facades: the backyards, the forgotten corners, the private domains. It is a record of the human structures we have made for ourselves over the centuries as well as of the life that we have led, of the way we have earned our living, of the way we have spent our leisure.

I was asked to select material that features Edinburgh and the life that people have led in this city. The choice of available images was overwhelming: one might rummage for a lifetime amongst the several million items in the collection. Guided by the curators, I have tried to choose photographs, engravings and images that tell the story of the city and capture in some way its essence. Much of what is shown in these photographs is still there, just as Edinburgh has retained its very distinctive character in a world that has become increasingly uniform. In a way this book is a love letter to a city. It is a love letter, though, in which the pictures do most of the speaking and the words are just the secondary tribute.

I am grateful to the staff of the Commission for all their help in guiding me through their marvellous archive. In particular I am grateful to James Crawford and Rebecca Bailey for their enthusiastic vision that a wider public should be able to appreciate the riches of this collection, and to Oliver Brookes, whose design has brought these fascinating images to life.

Browsing the RCAHMS Search Room, 2014

To look through the RCAHMS archive is to slip into the many layers of Scotland's past. Every photograph, map or engraving has a story to tell. I have used this material to tell a story of Edinburgh. It is by no means definitive, but that is the joy of how we respond to images of places that are dear to us. And while this is my story of Edinburgh, I hope it will resonate with all who hold the city close to their heart. RCAHMS DP195531

A Work

# of Beauty

I love this city, and always shall.

I write about it. I dream about it. I walk its streets and see something new each day – traces of faded lettering on the stone, still legible, but just; some facade that I have walked past before and either not noticed or not looked at closely enough; an unregarded doorway with the names, in brass, of those who lived there sixty years ago, the bell-pulls sometimes still in place, as if one might summon long-departed residents from their slumbers; a slice of sky that suddenly reveals itself through an archway; some pokey café or bar out of which wafts a hint of coffee beans or beer; an odd section of railings standing like a line of spears, or a small ironwork balcony dignified, perhaps, by fleurs-de-lys. Every day this city can reveal something old that is for me, in a sense, something new.

I first lived in Edinburgh as a student. It was then, as it still is, a wonderful place to lead the student life, a city every bit as romantic as Heidelberg or Bologna, or any of the other great university cities of Europe. The University of Edinburgh then occupied a significant part of the south side of the city. At its heart was the Old College on South Bridge, set about its generous quadrangle, with its magnificent Playfair Library. This was the seat of the Faculty of Law, and in its lecture halls, with their steeply raked floors and their highly uncomfortable wooden benches, I listened to lectures by gowned professors. Students bought newspapers in those days, and we would read these discreetly in the duller lectures or catch up on sleep. Between lectures, or at lunchtime, we went to the café at the back of the Museum next door. We bought pots of tea there and greasy mutton pies with baked beans. Healthy eating was yet to be invented.

The stone staircases of the Old College were worn down in the middle by the tread of countless student feet. The building reeked of history. In the basement, it was said, there was a trapdoor through which bodies were brought for dissection by the medics. Burke and Hare, of course, had pursued their dreadful trade just down the hill, in the slums of the Cowgate. On a misty night, one might still imagine their shades in the dark closes and entries. We knew, too, that this building had been built on the very spot, Kirk O'Fields, where Henry Darnley, husband of Mary Queen of Scots, had been murdered – blown into the air so high that he landed far from the bed he had occupied that evening. And in a corner of the building were the rooms of the Speculative Society, where Walter Scott and Robert Louis Stevenson, along with so many other Scottish luminaries, had met by candlelight to read each other essays and discuss the topics of the day. The Edinburgh of their time was full of societies like that, and still is. Robert Burns was a member of one.

The law students had their own favourite bar, the Captains Bar in College Street, shared with the locals who lived in the nineteenth century tenements that still dominated that part of the city. It was a long, narrow bar,

Calton Road looking up to Waterloo Place, c1950

Light and architecture cooperate in Edinburgh to an extraordinary extent. Perhaps this is because the light here comes to us at such acute angles. With the sun always directly overhead, Edinburgh would be a very different city.
H D Wylie, RCAHMS SCI124664

Bell Pulls, Marchmont, 2014

The front door of an Edinburgh tenement stair can be like a palimpsest (one of my favourite words, usually used of a document that has been written over many times). The names on the bell pulls often remain well after the occupants have moved on. When a bell was rung, residents could pull a lever on the landing to open the main door to let their visitor in. It was an effective mechanism of which Heath Robinson, that famous artist of unlikely contraptions, would have approved.

RCAHMS DPI94404

the walls lined with those decorated brewers' mirrors that gave old-fashioned bars such character. I remember taking a visiting French law student there one evening and hearing at first hand of the events he had just witnessed in Paris. It was 1968, and Paris was experiencing what seemed to be a revolution. Our visitor had thrown no cobble-stones himself, although he had witnessed the events. It was a long way from sedate Edinburgh.

A few blocks away was, and still is, fortunately, the McEwan Hall, a great round statement of a nineteenth century brewing magnate's munificence. Inside are classical murals: Greek youths sit at the feet of toga-clad philsophers. *Wisdom*, says the legend painted above, *is the principal thing: therefore get wisdom*. We sat examinations in there and were encouraged, perhaps, by that exhortation. And it was there that the installation of the University's rectors took place, accompanied by the singing of that most poignant of student songs, the 'Gaudeamus'. To the side of the McEwan Hall was the Men's Union (in those days they still had separate student facilities), a spiky gothic palace of dining rooms, rowdy bars, a library and a debating chamber that went sharply downmarket at weekends to become the Union Palais dance-hall. Here male students met young women training as nurses or studying at Atholl Crescent's college of domestic science – fondly, but rudely, called the Dough School. Attitudes were different then; students smoked in libraries, the men wore ties and jackets, and everybody

was less worldly-wise, less mature than they are today. It was, I suppose, rather an innocent time.

My student life was lived mostly in the Old Town and the South Side of the city. Later on, I moved to the rather more Bohemian area of Stockbridge, where I bought my first flat, which was small and part of a rather undistinguished tenement. It was solidly built, though, as much of nineteenth century Edinburgh was, and for all its lack of distinction it had a floor of fine broad Canadian pine that, when sanded and sealed, lent brightness to the rooms.

I frequented a coffee bar that had been set up in a building called Duncan's Land, one of the city's oldest houses; I had meals in a restaurant on one side of St Stephen's Street, a street of antique dealers and craftsmen, and met friends in a bar on the other side. I used to go running with a friend along the walkway that follows the Water of Leith from Stockbridge up to the Dean Village. We ran past the temple to Hygena and then under the towering Dean Bridge to the weir and millpond beyond. There was a very peaceful looking house, with a very large window, overlooking that bit of the river – a house that I learned belonged to the Polish artist Alexander Zyw. Not far away, clinging to the face of the cliff, was a house that seemed to grow out of the bare rock, a seemingly impossible feat of architecture. Here, more than anywhere else in the city, it may be brought home to anybody who is prepared to crane his or her neck, that this is a place that has never been inhibited by hills and ridges.

Those maps of our private world ...

After I married, we went up in the world and moved to Cumberland Street, in the Georgian New Town. A more expensive flat generally means more light: this was a lovely, airy flat with those pleasing Georgian proportions that make the New Town so agreeable a place to live. A few years later we moved to a house on the other side of town, near Napier University, acquiring what some architectural historians slightly disparagingly call a Victorian villa. That is where we remain, in a street of other Victorian villas.

Inevitably, if one spends many years in a city, particularly in a city one loves, there will be places within that city that have very strong associations – memories linked with a room, a building, a street or a corner. In one of the 44 Scotland Street novels, *Love over Scotland*, Angus Lordie, an artist who is given to philosophical reflections about the city, composes and recites a poem in which he considers the meaning of place. The poem starts with some observations on maps, but then moves on to the contemplation of how places in cities may trigger memories:

On the Subject of Maps
Although they are useful sources
Of information we cannot do without,
Regular maps have few surprises: their contour lines
Reveal where the Andes are, and are reasonably clear
On the location of Australia, and the Outer Hebrides;
Such maps abound; more precious, though,
Are the unpublished maps we make ourselves,
Of our city, our place, our daily world, our life;
Those maps of our private world
We use every day; here I was happy, in that place
I left my coat behind after a party,
This is where I met my love; I cried there once,
I was heart-sore; but felt better round the corner
Once I saw the hills of Fife across the Forth,
Things of that sort, our personal memories,
That make the private tapestry of our lives ...

West Railway Footbridge, Princes Street Gardens, 1949
The child in this photograph would have remembered this bridge and this moment when he was older. He would have remembered looking through the iron railings to the train tracks below, and gazing up at the castle, impossibly high to him.
Tom and Sybil Gray, RCAHMS SC679100

But it is not just personal associations that make a city for us, important though those may be: it is the spirit of the place, a difficult-to-define quality that gives a town or city, or indeed a stretch of countryside, its particular character. London and New York are the places they are because of … what? Immediately the images come to mind: the Thames curving round the Embankment, Trafalgar Square, flags along the Mall; or the Chrysler Building, the Empire State, a line of yellow cabs crawling up a stretched-out urban canyon. But images such as these, now so familiar as to have become clichés, are not the things that give a city its real feel: that is a much more complex matter and can really only be understood if we scrape away at today's picture of a city to see how it came to be what it was. This is how we reach a real understanding of a place – by finding out why it was there, and how it grew. This process also serves to underline the difference between a city of real character – a living city – and a city that is just a place for people to sleep and work. The city of character will have grown organically, usually over a long period, responding to the highly individual needs of time and place; it may be messy, it may be higgledy-piggledy, but there will be no mistaking its liveliness. Kolkatta is a vibrantly real city, or so I felt when I visited it; so are New York and Naples. An artificially created city, or a city that has grown too quickly, will not have a sense of organic growth. It will lack soul. It will not be a place that makes people fall in love with it, even those who visit it for a short time, or those who do not visit it

at all, but merely read about it or see pictures. The great cities of this world are loved, I suspect, by many who may never have the chance to see them. Venice has many lovers, but not all of them have set foot there. Venice is a dream to them, and Edinburgh, too, may be just that for some – a place they have seen depicted in photographs and wish to visit some day; we all have places like that in our lives.

The notion of organic growth of human settlements is one that has been explored at length by the visionary architect Christopher Alexander. Alexander is a professor of architecture who has devoted his career to developing a theory of humane building in which the buildings and towns in which we lead our lives are living entities rather than dead, impersonal creations. A city, he has argued, should consist of inter-related centres of human activity that speak to one another. A single building should not dominate those around it, should not seek to make an egotistical statement. New buildings should arise in response to real human needs rather than to grandiloquent visions of what the architects and planners feel we should want. Above all, the scale of our buildings should be personal – should not dwarf the human, should not destroy our inbuilt sense of the scale with which we feel comfortable.

I have long been an admirer of Christopher Alexander's views of what makes for a good place. I believe that Edinburgh has, through historical good fortune, been able to fulfil this vision, and that is why, I think, so many people fall in love with this city on their first visit. They feel *right* here, because the place *is* right. But why is it right? Why is it such a heart-breakingly engaging city? Why do we love it so? I think that the answer lies in how and when it grew and the uses to which, over the generations, we have put it; it also lies in nature and light and in the very particular nature of the Scottish culture that has spawned it. All of this went into a mix that has produced a place of fragile and entrancing beauty; a place that intrigues and seduces; a place that stands out as one of the loveliest cities in our world.

It began, of course, with geology. Cities often grow up because the topography is right: a well-placed hill, or hills, may be the lure for human settlement, just as may be a navigable river. Glasgow is on an important river, as is Inverness; Edinburgh's river is small, in dry weather not much more than a burn, but it has a wonderful natural advantage in the shape of the hill upon which its castle was built. An eminently defensible site, the Castle Rock dominates the countryside around it, and it was this feature that made Edinburgh, like Stirling, an attractive place for a town to establish itself. It was down the ridge that links the Castle with Holyrood that the Old Town developed and became the crowded, bustling city that provided the backdrop to many centuries of dramatic Scottish history. This is the Edinburgh Old Town – the name it still bears today to distinguish it from the Georgian New Town, built a stone's throw to the north.

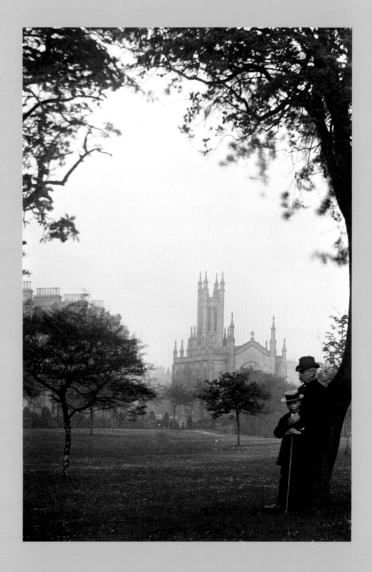

Belgrave Crescent Gardens and Holy Trinity Church, c1910
Certain streets in Edinburgh have their own gardens for the use of the local residents. These are sometimes rather secret places, from which one may look out onto the public face of the city – in this case a wonderfully ornate church, which stands guard at the north end of the Dean Bridge.
Francis M Chrystal, RCAHMS SC1098330

The Old Town is the very heart of Edinburgh – even today the place that more than anywhere else gives Scotland's capital its soul and character. Its origins can be traced back to the twelfth century, when King David I of Scotland founded the royal burgh of Edinburgh. Over the following centuries, walls circumscribing the town were built to embrace the closes (courtyard-like lanes) that led off the High Street, and the population grew until it was bursting at the seams. The houses of the Old Town reflected the cramped conditions that geography dictated, with overhanging extensions and very little or no space between structures. This paucity of space led to the construction of multi-storey buildings – tenements – that were to become the characteristic domestic buildings of Scottish cities. These were the skyscrapers of their day – buildings that, for their time, represented a real feat of architecture. Little of this earlier period remains, as a combination of fire, new construction, and war destroyed almost everything of the early Old Town. Yet making one's way about the High Street today, one has no real sense of interruption: the surrounding buildings may date from the seventeenth or eighteenth centuries, or even later, but their connection with what went before is still quite tangible. Perhaps it is because they occupy the same footprint, are made of the same stone, or reflect the same vernacular architecture. Perhaps it is because the roads, the closes and markets are in much the same place as they always were that this sense of continuity is so strong; whatever it is,

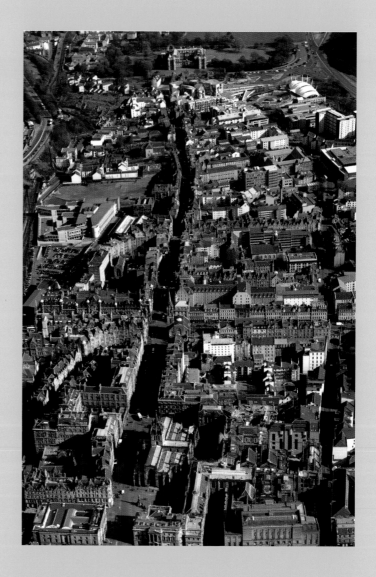

The Royal Mile, 2010
Picked out in shadow is the lower part of the spine that runs through the Old Town of Edinburgh. At the top of the picture we see Holyroodhouse and the Scottish Parliament – centres of old power and new power respectively.
RCAHMS DP075922

Here was crammed the whole life of the capital

no great leap of imagination is needed for the visitor to picture what it was like to live in this place four centuries or more ago.

Into the relatively small confines of the Old Town was crammed the whole life of the capital, from the royal court at one end of the spectrum to the world of the itinerant pedlar at the other. The business of state is symbolised by the Castle, still the city's dominant feature. Looking up at this rather daunting edifice from below – from Castle Terrace or King's Stables Road – one can imagine the sieges it has witnessed, and understand just how well-placed it was to repel these. This is architecture that is both symbolic and functional. It has been the nerve centre of a troubled and unsettled kingdom. It has been garrison and refuge. It has been the focal point of the hopes of dynasties. It has been a site of remembrance and worship. All of these human purposes have stamped themselves on a layout in which room is found for chapels, halls and kitchens as much as for barracks and magazines. Here are the history and concerns of the Scottish state set out before us. Here are the reminders of struggles and intrigues within Scotland and imperial adventures beyond its borders.

Closely bound up with the life of the Scottish state was the life of the Church. In contemporary secular society we forget how important and omnipresent religion was in the life of most Scots, governing daily life and giving rise to passions and commitments that seem extraordinary today.

Edinburgh was a religious battleground almost as much as it was a military one, and sermons and denunciations were probably far more common and fiery than political speeches. The physical reminders of this background are to be seen today in important churches such as St Giles' – the High Kirk, a stone or two of which date back to the twelfth century – Greyfriars Kirk, Holyrood Abbey and the Canongate Kirk. Three of these remain in use as churches, and not only continue to hold services but, in the hosting of concerts and talks, are still the living centres of community that they always were. The Old Town is not a museum; it is a place that continues to be lived and worked in, with people adapting ancient buildings to the needs of the day. Modern architectural renovation has let in light; glass has in places replaced stone; but the feel of the buildings, their tenacity and solidity, is much the same.

The main sites of trade and commerce were the markets that operated at a number of locations. The largest of these, the Grassmarket, occupies an important position in the shadow of the Castle, and is linked to the larger artery of George IV Bridge by Victoria Street, a curving, cobbled street of great charm. The small shops that survive here are like constructed caves in a hillside; external stone stairways climb up towards the Castle; a high promenade, a roof to the shops below, leads from the top of the street and then climbs the last few feet to the High Street above. One has a strong sense here of things built on top of other things, of commerce, and daily life, being carried out at different levels.

The Lawnmarket and St Giles' High Kirk, c1830

This engraving, from a collection titled 'Views in Scotland', shows the liveliness of the Old Town in the early nineteenth century. Residents, traders, kilted soldiers – and dogs – go about their affairs in a suspiciously pristine Lawnmarket. The main items for sale appear to be large bolts of tartan cloth. The smart attire of the shoppers suggests, however, that they are not buying tat.

Thomas H Shepherd, RCAHMS DP095408

A striking feature of Old Town life was its intimacy. Because people lived in such proximity to one another, there was not only a boisterous social life but there was also a greater mixing of social classes than occurred in cities where high and low were housed at some remove from one another. This gave Edinburgh a strong civic sense – something that it retains to this day and that may, perhaps, find its roots in the cheek by jowl social mix of the Old Town. A close, or courtyard, might house not only the Court of Session judge, the philosopher and the man of business, but also the man who sold these worthies their food or stabled their horses. The one building might contain hovels at ground level but more spacious and less malodorous flats further up the stair (where the air would certainly be better). This meant that the well-off could not ignore or avoid their fellow citizens in the way in which their equivalents who lived in more divided cities might do. Architecture obviously reflects the character of the culture it serves, but it may also mould it. If there is a strong tradition of egalitarianism in Scottish culture, then it is possible that it comes from the proximity within which all classes of people lived in Scottish cities.

Intimate it may have been, but the Old Town could also be described as crowded, insanitary and impractical. The author of an important 1752 pamphlet making the case for the expansion of the city paints a striking picture of just how bad things were.

The narrow lanes leading to north and south, by reason of their steepness, narrowness, and dirtiness, can only be considered as so many unavoidable nuisances. Confined by the small compass of the walls … the houses stand more crowded than in any other town in Europe, and are built to a height that is almost incredible. Hence necessarily follows a great want of free air, light, cleanliness, and every other comfortable accommodation. Hence also many families, sometimes no less than ten or a dozen, are obliged to live overhead of each other in the same building …'

The author of this pamphlet then goes on to remark that, as a result of all this, the city receives very few visitors and many

local prejudices and narrow notions, inconsistent with polished manners and growing wealth, are still so obstinately retained.

The tenor of these remarks is clear: the Old Town was just a bit too lived-in to meet the needs of a country that was becoming more prosperous and refined. And yet even if the Old Town was a teeming hive of markets and smells, of towering buildings and burrowing closes, it was also one of the great intellectual centres of Europe – the beating heart of the Scottish Enlightenment. The famous remark that at the time of the Enlightenment one could stand at the Mercat Cross in Edinburgh and shake hands with fifty men of genius was, of course, a gross exaggeration: at least some of the hands one shook would be those of pickpockets, or some of the odd and unusual characters immortalised in the barber-artist James Kay's magnificent *Edinburgh Portraits*. But some might well have been of the thinkers and writers who, for a brief period, made Edinburgh the intellectual capital of Europe. David Hume, perhaps the most influential of philsophers to write in the English language, lived in the Old Town in Riddle's Court in the Lawnmarket and later further down the Royal Mile in the Canongate. His close friend Adam Smith also lived in the Canongate, at Panmure House. Smith was the author of *An Inquiry into the Nature and Causes of the Wealth of Nations*, a work that is regarded as the foundation stone of the modern science of economics. The inventors of modern geology, James Hutton, and sociology, Adam Ferguson, also lived in Edinburgh at this time. All of these men may have lived in a small and rather cramped city, far to the north of Paris, Rome and London, but from their cold fastness on that ridge of rock in Scotland they changed the way the world thought about itself.

The Old Town was also the centre of a thriving literary society. If one walks past the Canongate Kirk today, half way down the Royal Mile towards the Palace of Holyroodhouse, one encounters, realistically placed on the pavement, the jaunty statue of Robert Fergusson, the poet whose work was a substantial influence on Robert Burns, and who is buried in the Kirkyard behind the statue. Fergusson died very young, but Burns himself was only in his late twenties when he came to Edinburgh, feted by the city's fashionable society after the publication of his collection of poems. Other writers followed: Walter Scott, who may be credited with the invention of the historical novel, and Stevenson were both authors who lived and worked in Edinburgh and for whom the Old Town was a haunt.

Edinburgh's centre of gravity may have shifted towards the end of the eighteenth century with the construction of the New Town, but the Old Town remained a vital, lived-in part of the city, housing the courts, the city administration, and numerous cultural and commercial concerns. The adaptation of centuries-old buildings to new purposes, without losing a sense of what these buildings originally were, has meant that the essential character of this marvellously atmospheric urban landscape has been preserved. The hustle and bustle is still there, as is the sense that just round the next corner something surprising and important is about to happen.

I like to walk along George IV Bridge, past the two large library buildings. On one side is Edinburgh Public Library, which on the outside today is perhaps

The National Library of Scotland, George IV Bridge, 1956

In Edinburgh, it is important to look up because a lot happens above eye level. Many people walk past the seven figures on the National Library's facade without seeing them. Produced by the sculptor Hew Lorimer – son of the architect Sir Robert Lorimer – they are intended to represent the 'Arts of Civilisation': history, law, medicine, music, poetry, science and theology.

The National Library is one of a handful of copyright libraries that must receive, by law, a copy of every book published in the United Kingdom. Not surprisingly, the collection has outgrown this wonderful building and many of its books are kept elsewhere.
Tom and Sybil Gray, RCAHMS SC680364

Who was the man who, day in day out, pored over bound copies of

somewhat dark and slightly foreboding. Like many libraries throughout the country, this was paid for by the great Scottish philanthropist Andrew Carnegie, who laid the foundation stone for this building himself. His bust greets you as you ascend the main staircase of this library, though most who walk past him today will be unaware of who he was. That is understandable enough; every age has its own great men and women and we replace our heroes and heroines with new ones. Yet it seems to me important that we should continue to put a human face to the places we occupy – so many buildings in Edinburgh have the fingerprints of those who created them still there, visible for those who care to look for them. Modern construction does not always have this: faceless works of glass and steel often say nothing about the people who made them or who caused them to be made.

On the other side of the street is the headquarters of the National Library of Scotland, a great sandstone building begun in the nineteen-thirties and finished in the fifties. The facade of the National Library is decorated with stone figures, recessed into the wall, representing the arts and professions. I used to spend time there as a postgraduate research student, sitting in the echoing reading room at long tables to which books would be brought up from the bowels of the building by attendants. Every great library has its denizens, and the National Library Reading Room was a great place for spotting curious people to whom the imagination might attribute colourful stories. Who, we

wondered, was the man who, day in day out, pored over old bound copies of the *Scotsman* newspaper, taking the occasional note in an ancient notebook? What nuggets of information was he seeking amidst those columns of births and deaths, those reports of sheriff court cases, those advertisements for cars and clothing? Who were the avid readers of tomes on Hebridean folklore or the history of poisons? What exactly did they have in mind? Card indices have been replaced by computers, but that was another period feature of the Reading Room – those beautiful trays of cards on which the details of the nation's treasure store of books were painstaking typed and occasionally annotated in ink.

Once you are past the libraries you are at one of the most important junctions of the High Street. This is pretty much the heart of Edinburgh, with St Giles' High Kirk on the other side of a large square that is just made for ceremonies. Next to St Giles' is the Signet Library, one of Edinburgh's triumphs of formal architecture. This library, which belongs to a legal society, the Society of Writers to the Signet, is reminiscent of the Playfair Library in Edinburgh University's Old College. It stretches off into the distance, bay after bay of books on each side. It is used for large meetings as well as for weddings and dances. I remember on one occasion attending a dinner in the Signet Library to mark an important anniversary of the Speculative Society of Edinburgh. Several hundred former members – known in the Society as Extraordinary Members – were there to

the Scotsman?

hear an extremely important guest give a speech. The poet Christopher Grieve, who wrote under the name of Hugh MacDiarmid and who was one of the principal figures of the Scottish literary renaissance of the second half of the twentieth century, was there as an Honorary Member of the Society. He had enjoyed – as was his habit – a certain amount of his favourite whisky, and found himself in disagreement with what the guest of honour had to say in his speech. MacDiarmid was not one to mince his words, and he began to barrack the speaker, who was not used to being treated in this way (he was, in fact, the Duke of Edinburgh), but who nonetheless took the interruptions in a very good-humoured way. Two members of the Society, however – a Court of Session judge and a sheriff – decided that it would be best if the poet were to be removed, and did so, picking him up and carrying him kicking and protesting from the room. Nobody was offended by the episode, which was very much in accordance with the Scottish tradition of direct speech. Scottish poets are famous for speaking their minds. Burns would have understood that scene, and appreciated it.

Diagonally across the square from the entrance to the Signet Library, the Scottish philosopher David Hume sits on his plinth. It is a good place for a statue of Hume to be: his grave is on Calton Hill, but here he is right in the middle of the city's life, caught in a suitably pensive mood by the distinguished contemporary sculptor Alexander Stoddart. This sculptor is also responsible for the statue of

James Clerk Maxwell, the Scottish physicist, outside the headquarters of the Royal Society of Edinburgh in George Street, and for the new figure of Clio, the muse of History, placed atop the Scottish National Portrait Gallery. Behind Hume, the road dips down to the Mound, the hill that slopes sharply to Princes Street and the New Town. Now there lies before you the great sweep of the New Town, the 'new' classical city that was built to escape the confines of the Old Town and that today constitutes one of the most edifying views afforded by any European city. It is so beautiful that people often are stopped in their tracks, as they absorb the sight of the roofs of Princes Street, the flags fluttering along the road and on top of the National Gallery, and the spiky surprise of the monument to Walter Scott. All of a sudden, one is in a different place. The Old Town, huddled and mysterious, becomes a sweep of elegant streets and squares, a living, inhabited monument to Palladian proportions, and to light, air and elegance.

The construction of the New Town followed the draining of the Nor Loch and the building of the North Bridge. Now came the plan – and it was drawn up by an architect who was just 22 years of age: James Craig. In his designs for the New Town we see Craig's desire for order and symmetry. Yet in spite of these objectives, it was not possible – at least in the first wave of construction – to achieve these goals as completely as Craig and others of his view wanted. This resulted from a number of factors, including complications in land ownership and the incorporation of

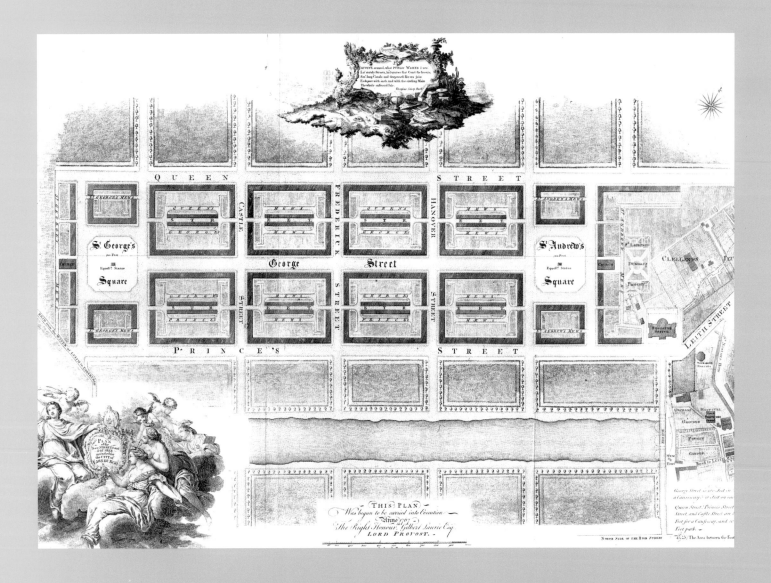

James Craig's Plan of the New Town of Edinburgh, 1767

A 22-year-old architect won the competition to design Edinburgh's second city. It was called, quite simply, the 'New Town', and this simplicity was also reflected in its plan – a wonderful example of geometric elegance. Craig, 'with the utmost humility', dedicated the plan in its inscription to 'his Most Sacred majesty, George III, The Munificent Patron of every polite and liberal Art'. It is to the eternal benefit of Edinburgh that King George approved of 'this Plan of the New Streets and Squares intended for his ancient capital of North Britain' before he went mad – James Craig, RCAHMS SC466310

buildings that were already there. Yet several parts of the New Town achieved a remarkable balance and harmony, somehow seeming to express in stone the Enlightenment philosophy of reason and restraint. If Hume and other philosophers of the Enlightenment were to make themselves a city, then it would be somehow like this; and Hume did, in fact, build himself a house on the edge of one of the most important Georgian squares, St Andrew's Square.

At the other end of George Street, Charlotte Square expressed the ideals of its architect, Robert Adam. This square is largely unchanged today, and when you stand at its entrance at the end of George Street you cannot but be struck by the perfect harmony of its south and north sides, by its dignity, by its understated elegance. There is nothing loud about Charlotte Square; it has all the restraint and harmony of a composition by Bach – it is a tangible expression of order. Similarly, just down the hill, the rather grand houses of Moray Place, all holding hands in a circle around the gardens in the centre, remind one of the miracle of control that has been achieved in much of the New Town. In so many other cities one finds architecturally striking streets and squares, but almost always changes have been made to disrupt whatever unified architectural vision there was at the beginning. People may have altered facades or painted houses different colours – there is virtually none of that in the Edinburgh New Town. Here strict feuing

conditions – the Scottish legal system's way of enforcing restrictions on what can be done with property – meant that the owners of buildings were obliged to respect limitations on alterations or deviations from the original conception. It is one of the most striking features of the New Town that there are such large areas of visual unity: few jarring notes have crept in.

Not everybody approved of this austere classicism. The author and historian Allan Massie in his book on Edinburgh reminds us of some of that criticism:

> The Old Town, it is argued, correctly, was a higgledy-piggledy, socially heterogeneous place; the building of the New Town introduced new social divisions to Edinburgh. Gradually the Old Town was abandoned to the poor, while the prosperous bourgeoisie ensconced themselves in the sedate squares and bland streets of the New. An American who visited the city in 1834 remarked that 'Paris is not more unlike Constantinople than one side of Edinburgh is unlike the other.'

Even if Heriot Row and Moray Place may have always provided housing for the wealthy and the privileged, they were not as far removed from the homes of the poor and disadvantaged. Immediately behind Heriot Row was Jamaica Place, which was considerably more modest, and Moray Place, although elevated above Stockbridge, was not all that far from the latter's very unassuming back streets. Indeed in some parts of the New Town, such as Cumberland Street and Scotland Street, the social mix during the twentieth century was quite different from that which one would encounter in the more gentrified streets of the New Town. It was for this reason that I chose Scotland Street as the background for my series of novels of that name: I wanted a setting that would enable me to inject an element of Bohemianism into the lives of a group of New Town residents. Scotland Street was perfect for that. And there were so many places close to it that had strong literary associations. Compton Mackenzie, the author of *Whisky Galore* and other well-known twentieth century Scottish novels, lived in Drummond Place, just round the corner from the top end of Scotland Street, as did Sydney Goodsir Smith, the poet. From the same flat in which he wrote, Compton Mackenzie also ran the affairs of the British Siamese Cat Society – a juxtaposition that says something about the glorious eccentric spirit of Edinburgh. On the other side of Drummond Place Gardens, where Nelson Street joins the square, lived another poet who celebrated Edinburgh, Robert Garioch. Garioch was adept at portraying the pretensions of the Edinburgh establishment – his poem *Did you See Me?* is in my view every bit as powerful a tilt at pomposity as Robert

Burns's *Holy Willie's Prayer*. In this poem, Garioch is a civic dignitary who goes to an official, outdoor occasion, only to be mocked by the *keelies* (rough elements) of the town, who get wind of the affair. The final line is a marvellously poignant confession of over-dressing: *I'm awfu sorry I wore my MA goon*. (I'm awfully sorry I wore my MA gown.)

My own favourite Edinburgh view may be glimpsed not far from Scotland Street and Drummond Place. This is the view that lies before you as you walk down Dundas Street. Like many Edinburgh views, it changes by the minute, depending on what the weather is doing ('Edinburgh,' the American writer Cheryl Mendelson once remarked to me, 'is a very *weathery* city'). If visibility is good, you see, at the end of the street and over the roofs of the houses, the hills of Fife on the other side of the Firth of Forth. The hillsides change colour with the season: steely grey in mid-winter; perhaps, suddenly green and glowing on a fine spring day; brown and yellow under ripened crops in the fullness of summer. And above them a sky that is at one moment white with low cloud, or purple with rain, or sliced by shafts of golden sunlight. No city, I think, could wish for a more beautiful backdrop. We may complain about our changeable weather and long for the constancy of a Mediterranean sky, but our sky is an integral part of the show, the gorgeous stage-curtains that hang above this opera-set of a city.

**The Lawnmarket and Edinburgh Castle,
from the Tower of St Giles' High Kirk, c1938**
This is a very unusual but extremely striking view of the Lawnmarket with the Castle in the distance. Today we might think that the mistiness is mist. In fact, it looks as if it is smoke. Edinburgh's nickname has long been Auld Reekie, a comment on the effect of coal fires. Smoke blackened the city's stone, but increasingly the accumulated soot and grime is being washed away, and the true colour of Edinburgh is returning – RCAHMS SC1102951

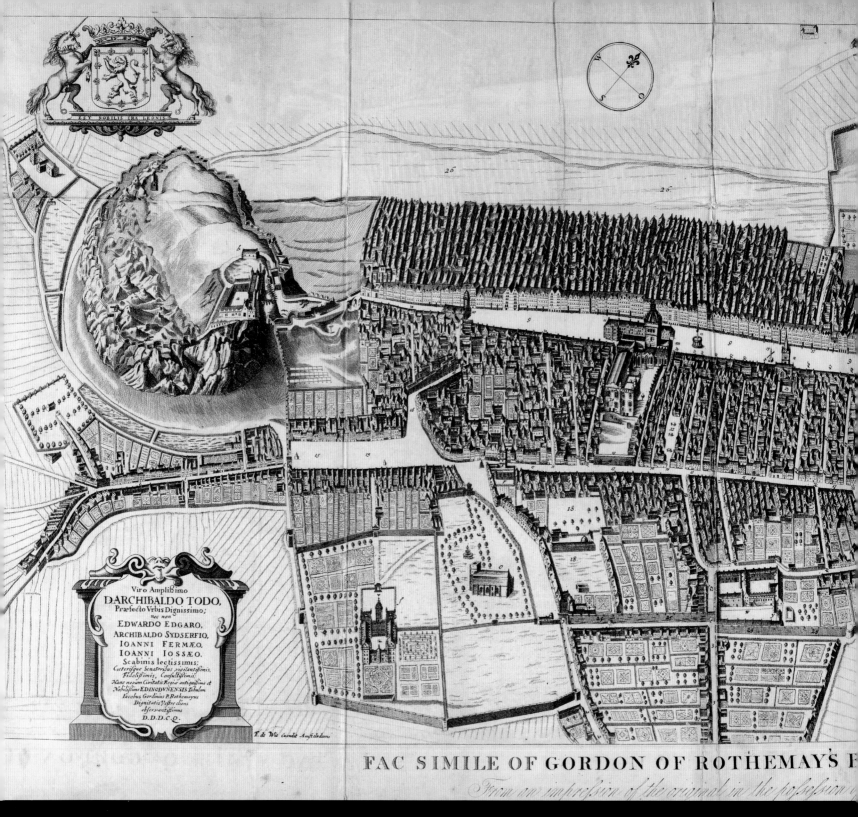

Viro Ampliſsimo
D ARCHIBALDO TODO,
Præfecto Vrbis Dignissimo;
nec non
EDWARDO EDGARO.
ARCHIBALDO SYDSERFIO.
IOANNI FERMÆO.
IOANNI IOSSÆO.
Scabinis lectissimis;
Ceterisque Senatoribus vigilantissimis,
Fidelissimis, Consultissimis,
Hanc novam Civitatis Regiæ antiquissimæ et
Nobilissimæ EDINODVNENSIS Tabulam
Iacobus Gordinius P. Rothemoyus
Dignitatis Veſtræ cliens
observantissimus
D.D.D.C.Q.

F. de Wit Excudit Amſtelodami.

FAC SIMILE OF GORDON OF ROTHEMAY'S P

From our impreſſion of the original in the poſſeſſion

James Gordon of Rothiemay's Bird's Eye View of Edinburgh, 1647

Just like the famous seventeenth century panorama of London produced by the Bohemian etcher Wenceslaus Hollar, this elaborate drawing remains one of the most popular and well-known views of Edinburgh. It was the work of

James Gordon, the fifth son of Robert Gordon of Straloch. James was a pastor by profession, with a sideline in cartography. By imagining the city from above – a vantage point that was of course impossible at the time – he succeeded in

capturing its innate character. The Old Town was a tightly compressed place, with only one main street, hemmed in on all sides by towering tenements. In essence and feel, this is how it remains today.

James Gordon of Rothiemay, RCAHMS SC759018

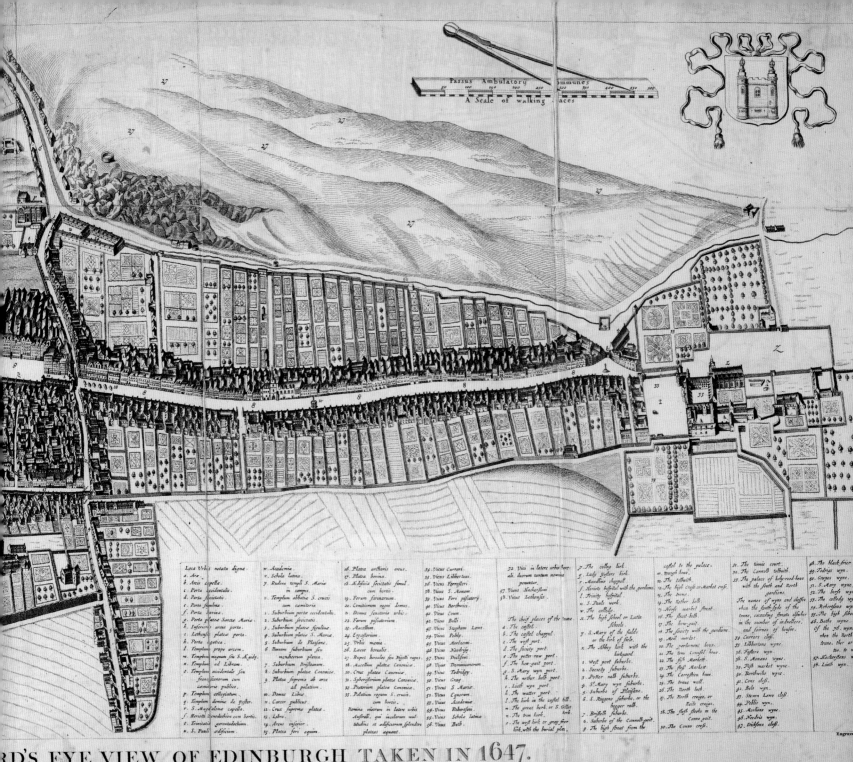

Passus Ambulatory Communes
50 100 150 200 250 300 350 400 450 500
A Scale of walking paces

Loca Urbis notatu digna.	w. *Academia.*	16. *Platea archioris arcus.*	34. *Vicus Curreri.*	72. *Vici in latere urbis bore-*
a. *Arx.*	x. *Schola latina.*	17. *Platea bovina.*	35. *Vicus Libbertous.*	*ale ducrum tantum nomine*
b. *Arcis capella.*	y. *Rudera templi S. Maria*	18. *Ædificia societatis simul*	36. *Vicus Fgresleri*	*ponuntur.*
c. *Porta occidentalis.*	*in campis*	*cum hortis.*	38. *Vicus S. Monani.*	57. *Vicus Sucherstoni*
d. *Porta societatis.*	z. *Templum abbate S. crucis*	19. *Forum farinarum.*	39. *Vicus Fori piscatoria*	58. *Vicus Lethensis.*
e. *Porta figulina.*	*cum camiterio*	20. *Comitiorum regni domus.*	40. *Vicus Com.*	
f. *Porta bovina.*	1. *Suburbium porta occidentalis.*	21. *Domus senatoria urbis*	42. *Vicu Belli.*	*The chief places of the toune.*
g. *Porta platea Sancte Maria.*	2. *Suburbium societatis*	22. *Macellum.*	43. *Vicus Stephan Lawt.*	a. *The castel.*
h. *Inferioris arcus porta.*	3. *Suburbium platea figuline*	24. *Ergasterium.*	44. *Vicus Pebly.*	b. *The castel chappel.*
i. *Letheris platea porta.*	4. *Suburbium platea S. Maria*	25. *Urbis mania.*	45. *Vicus Morleom.*	c. *The west port.*
k. *Porta aqatica.*	5. *Suburbium de Plaisane.*	26. *Lacus borealis.*	46. *Vicus Needry.*	d. *The society port.*
l. *Templum prope arcem.*	6. *Ilnnam suburbium seu*	27. *Rupes boreales seu Nigelli rupes*	47. *Vicus Dicksoni.*	e. *The potter-raw port.*
m. *Templum magnu feu S. Ægidy.*	*mendictorum platea*	28. *Macellum platea Canonice.*	48. *Vicus Dominicanorum*	f. *The how-gait port.*
n. *Templum ad Librum.*	7. *Suburbium Brisloanum.*	30. *Crux platea Canonice.*	49. *Vicus Todriday.*	g. *S. Mary wyn port.*
o. *Templum occidentale seu*	8. *Suburbium platea Canonice.*	32. *Sphersterium platea Canonice.*	50. *Vicus Gray.*	h. *The nether bell port.*
franciscanorum cum	9. *Platea suprema ab arce*	34. *Pretorium platea Comnice.*	51. *Vicus S. Maria.*	1. *Lieth wyn port.*
camiterio publice.	*ad palatium.*	35. *Palatium regum S. crucis,*	52. *Vicus Equorum.*	k. *The watter port.*
p. *Templum collegiatum.*	10. *Domus Libre.*	*cum hortis.*	53. *Vicus Academa*	l. *The kirk in the castel hill.*
q. *Templum domine de Jester.*	11. *Carcer publicut.*	*Nomina vicorum in latere urbis*	54. *Vicus Robertsoni*	m. *The great kerk, or S. Gilet*
r. *S. Magdalena capella.*	12. *Crux suprema platea.*	*Australi, qui incolarum mul-*	55. *Vicus Schola latina*	*kerk.*
ſ. *Heroti Xenodochien cum horti.*	13. *Libra.*	*titudine et adificiorum splendore*	56. *Vicus Beth.*	n. *The tron kerk.*
t. *Trinitatis gerontodochium.*	14. *Arcus inferior.*	*plateas aquant.*		o. *The west kerk or grey fra*
u. *S. Pauli ædificium.*	15. *Platea fori equum.*			*kirk, with the burial plat.*

p. *The colleg kirk*	*castel to the palace.*	31. *The tinnie court.*
q. *Lady Yesters kirk.*	w. *trough hous.*	32. *The Cannels tolbuith.*
r. *Maudlins chappell.*	12. *The tolbuith.*	33. *The palace of holy-rood-hous*
s. *Heriots hospital with the gardins.*	12. *The high Crosse or Market cross*	*with the fouth and North*
t. *Trinitie hospital*	13. *The trone*	*gardins.*
u. *S. Pauls work.*	14. *The nether tolb.*	*The names of wyns and closses*
w. *The colledge*	15. *Marek market street*	*when the south syde of the*
x. *S. Mary of the fields*	16. *The strait-kirk-*	*toune, exceeding streats elsher*
or the kirk of field.	17. *The bow-gait.*	*in the number of indwellers.*
z. *The Abbey kirk with the*	18. *The society with the gardines*	*and fairnes of houses.*
kirkyaird.	19. *Meil market*	34. *Curreri closs.*
1. *west port suburbs*	20. *The parlament hous.*	35. *Libbertons wyne.*
2. *Society suburbs*	21. *The toun Counsell hous.*	36. *Fosters wyn*
3. *Potter rath suburbs*	22. *The fish Markett*	38. *S. Monans wyne.*
4. *St. Mary wyn suburbs*	23. *The Corresthon hous*	39. *Fish market wyne.*
5. *Suburbs of Plaisane.*	24. *The toune wall*	40. *Borthwiks wyne.*
6. *S. Ringeons suburbs, or the*	25. *The North loch.*	41. *Coms closs.*
begger rath	26. *The North croags, or*	42. *Belo wyne.*
7. *Brisolk suburbs.*	*Neils croaas.*	43. *Steven Lowe closs*
8. *Suburbs of the Cannoll-gait*	28. *The flesh stocks in the*	44. *Pebls wyne.*
9. *The high streat from the*	*Canno gait.*	45. *Aorlions wyne*
	30. *The Canno cross*	46. *Needris wyn.*
		47. *Dicksns closs.*

48. *The black frier*
Todrigs wyn
49. *Gowyes wyne.*
51. *S. Mary wyne*
52. *The boro wyn.*
53. *The colledg wy*
54. *Robertsons wyne*
55. *The high school*
56. *Beths wyne*
Of the 56. wyns
when the North
toune, ther ar
two. to w
57. *Sucherstons*
58. *Lieth wyn.*

Engrave

RD'S EYE VIEW OF EDINBURGH TAKEN IN 1647.
Duncan Coran Esq. one of the Magistrates of the City

Published by Kirkwood & Son Edinburgh & Wm. Faden Charing Cross London 1817.

The Prospect of Edinburgh from ye North

most striking are the long gardens which can be seen
running off the slopes of the Old Town, *rus in urbe*,
soon to be built over as the city expanded.
John Slezer, RCAHMS SC1245640

left
Views of Edinburgh, 1868 and c1829

This is a city that cannot help but impress from
a distance. Top left we see a view from the
south-east looking over the picturesque ruin of
St Anthony's Chapel, to an almost bewildering
accumulation of hills, valleys, spires, towers
and bridges. Bottom left, with a shepherd
approaching Edinburgh from the exact opposite
direction, we see the refined frontage of the New
Town, punctuated elegantly at its west end by the
dome of St George's Church. Beyond are the Old
Town and the great bulk of Arthur's Seat.
top left – RCAHMS DP033103
bottom left – Thomas H Shepherd,
RCAHMS DP029336

above
Craigleith Quarry, 1829

As the caption to this nineteenth century
engraving explains, this was the stone quarry
'from which the New Town was built'. Large
portions of the city – and indeed, of other cities
around the world – were put together from the
famously durable building blocks of Craigleith
sandstone.
Thomas H Shepherd, RCAHMS DP094216

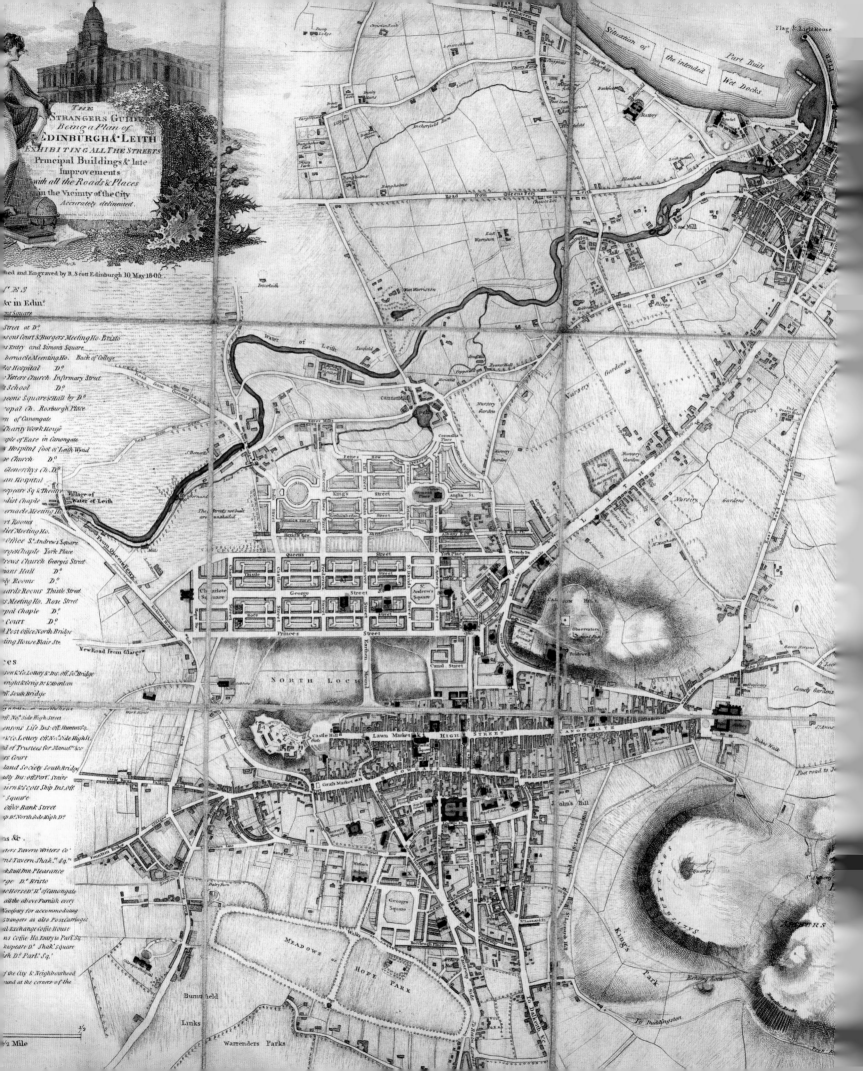

left
Map of Edinburgh, 1805
This rather attractive engraving is titled the
'Strangers' Guide' to Edinburgh and Leith. It
is a good name for a map, getting to the heart
of what all maps are about – helping those
who are new to a city to move around their
surroundings with confidence. Here we see
clearly the contrast between the organic Old
Town and planned New Town. Winding from
left to right across the page is the bright blue
ribbon of the Water of Leith. And marked in
red on the map, so the key tells us, are all the
'Principal Builidings and late improvements
with all the roads and places in the vicinity of
the City accurately delineated'. At this time,
of course, parts of the New Town would still
have been under construction. At a time of
rapid urban growth, new maps must have been
drawn constantly to keep up.
Robert Scott, RCAHMS DP149771

right
**Edinburgh Castle from the
Grassmarket, c1940**
Some things, however, do not change. While
the city has grown around it, the Castle has
remained Edinburgh's focal point.
B C Clayton, RCAHMS SC1122095

The Mercat Cross and the High Street, 1869

The unicorn in this photograph sits on the top of the Mercat Cross. Today, this curious structure is a composite of fragments of former Mercat Crosses that stood on or around this same spot at the civic heart of Edinburgh. In 1756 much of the original was destroyed because it had been, for many years, blamed for obstructing traffic (inlcuding a great procession for James VI in 1617 on his return to Scotland after uniting the crowns). A century later, Walter Scott showed his pique at this callous treatment of the monument in his epic poem *Marmion*:

But now is razed that monument
Whence royal edict rang
and voice of Scotland's law was sent
In glorious trumpet clang
Oh! Be his tomb as lead to lead
Upon its dull destroyer's head.

Thanks to campaigners like Scott, the cross was rebuilt in the later nineteenth century and is now in use once again for civic purposes – it is from this spot, for instance, that the Lord Lyon announces the prorogation of Parliament.

Royal Incorporation of Architects in Scotland, RCAHMS SC801639

West Bow and
George Heriot's School, c1800

This engraving from the beginning of the
nineteenth century reveals an important feature
of the Old Town – the various levels at which life
was lived. The West Bow descends here to the
Grassmarket. Rising above the tenements we
have, in the distance, the imposing structure of
George Heriot's School.
Thomas Dick, RCAHMS SC934255

Edinburgh Castle and the Grassmarket, viewed from the west end of the Cowgate, 1950

On any walk through Edinburgh one will see views framed by other buildings. It is one of the great appeals of the city for those exploring it on foot. To my eyes, such views are reminiscent of Dutch paintings of the seventeenth century, in which it was a common artistic device to look from one place into another. This is a city that is at once narrow and expansive, where sky, architecture, hills and sea can always be seen – sometimes in a glimpse, other times in a sweeping panorama.
Tom and Sybil Gray, RCAHMS SC679139

Waverley Bridge and Princes Street from the foot of Cockburn Street, c1920
RCAHMS SC1061262

Looking down Tron Square to Guthrie Street and Chambers Street, 1947

This view of Edinburgh no longer exists, cut off by building works in the second half of the twentieth century. Past the clock – which has now been moved to the Tron Square – we can just see Chambers Street in the distance, and the elevated bridge linking the Old College to the National Museum of Scotland.

Tom and Sybil Gray, RCAHMS SC679092

Guthrie Street looking over the Cowgate to Tron Square, c1930

Francis M Chrystal, RCAHMS SC1098288

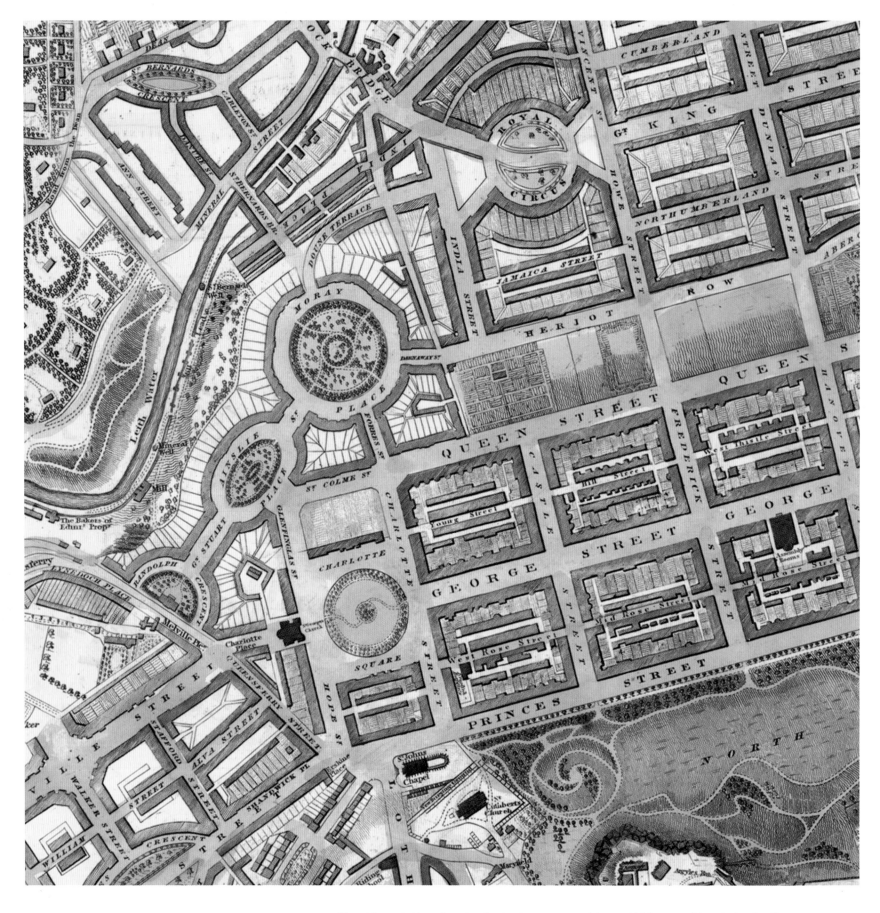

Plan of the City of Edinburgh, including all the latest and intended improvements, 1831

Plans – when applied on the ground – do not always work: the end result may look rather different from what is envisaged on the drawing board. The New Town of Edinburgh is an exception – it looks exactly as it should. The aerial photograph on the right shows the elegant sweep of the New Town's streets and its lovely crescents and circuses. While some of these look rather like crop circles, they were the creation of a classical rather than an alien intelligence.

Thomas Brown, National Library of Scotland, Licensor Scran

Aerial photograph of the New Town, 1988

Copyright Getmapping plc

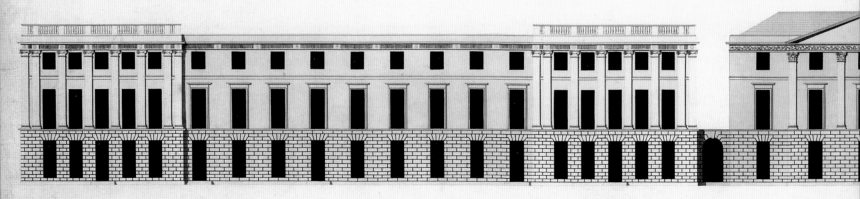

Design Elevation West Si[de]

Scale of

The West Side of Charlotte Square, c1800

The beauty of Charlotte Square lies in its regularity. There is a calm classical rationality in its design, captured in this beautiful elevation drawing from the beginning of the nineteenth century. The harmony of its architecture was explicit and deliberate.

In 1791, Edinburgh's Lord Provost invited Robert Adam, one of Scotland's greatest ever architects, to design a square that was 'not much ornamented, but with an elegant simplicity'. Adam fulfilled his brief magnificently.

George Heriot's Trust, RCAHMS DP137460

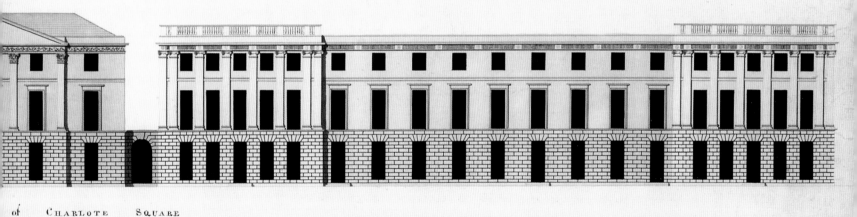

of CHARLOTE SQUARE

8 Queen Street, Royal College of Physicians, c1770

This elevation drawing of No. 8 Queen Street was also the work of Robert Adam. Here again, Adam used his mastery of classical techniques to create a sober and refined frontage for what was originally one large, individual house. It also set a standard

for the street which other architects struggled to match. In 1845, the Royal College of Physicians took up residence at No. 9 next door, and then in the mid-twentieth century the two buildings were joined together. RCAHMS SC1027555

House for the architect James Peddie, Lansdowne Crescent, c1864

Terraced houses in the New Town were designed in a grand style that is found in few other places in the world. This elevation shows a house for the renowned architect James Peddie of the firm Dick, Peddie and McKay. Lansdowne Crescent forms one side of one of the New Town's elegant ellipses: shapes formed by two curved rows of terraced houses facing each other across a central space of trees and gardens – Dick Peddie and McKay, RCAHMS DP089185

The east end of George Street, 1829

St Andrew's Square, which we can glimpse here
at the east end of George Street, was associated
with banking and finance, and still is to an extent.
The church on the left is St Andrew's and
St George's, which remains in use for religious
services today. This nineteenth century engraving
emphasises the elegance of George Street through
the figures promenading on the pavements. The
women are wearing expensive bonnets and the
men mounted on horses ride with confidence.
Nobody here is thinking of financial crashes.
Thomas H Shepherd, RCAHMS DP095262

The west end of George Street, 1829

The opposite end of George Street is captured
in another engraving suggestive of prosperity and
confidence. Beyond the uniform facades of the
street's buildings – outside of which wait horses
and carriages to transport wealthy residents – is
Charlotte Square and the impressive bulk of
St George's Church. In the 1960s, St George's
became West Register House. One of several
repositories for the National Records of Scotland,
it today holds an archive of documents preserving
a great deal of the nation's memory.
Thomas H Shepherd, RCAHMS DP095406

previous pages

Heriot Row

In contrast to the hustle and bustle of the Old Town, the New Town was to be clean, uncluttered and able to breathe. Heriot Row is one of the most elegant of New Town streets – but its architecture is, nonetheless, recognisably domestic in spite of the grandeur. These are houses in which families lived, and still do. Robert Louis Stevenson lived at number 17, and it was the distinctive wrought-iron lamppost outside his front door that inspired him to write his well-known poem 'Leerie the Lamplighter'. Stevenson imagined a young boy pressing up against his Heriot Row window to watch a man – Leerie – come 'with lantern and ladder' to ignite the city's gas lamps one after the other. His father may have been a banker and 'as rich as he can be', but the boy's only ambition when he was older was to join Leerie on his rounds of Edinburgh. I'm not sure that his banker father would have endorsed this career path.

top left

Looking east along Heriot Row, 1957

Tom and Sybil Gray, RCAHMS SC680438

bottom left

View of numbers 1 to 19, Heriot Row, c1950

RCAHMS SC502945

top right

Looking west along Heriot Row, c1950

RCAHMS SC502779

bottom right

Charlotte Square, 1956

Tom and Sybil Gray, RCAHMS SC679844

right

Heriot Row, 2014

The fanlights above these doors are quite beautiful – as is the associated stonework. This photograph is a perfect illustration of the simplicity and regularity which lay at the heart of the New Town's aesthetic. The recessed doors invite one in, whereas, at the same time, the unadorned plain steps say that garish ostentation is not welcome. Repetition plays a major part in the overall effect. RCAHMS DP195014

Moray Place, at the junction with Doune Terrace, 1957

Designed by James Gillespie Graham in 1827 for the Earl of Moray, Moray Place is generally considered to be the grandest of the New Town's circuses; this is Edinburgh at its most elegant and confident. Today these large houses are usually flatted, but when used as single dwellings they provided spacious and impressive townhouses for the well-to-do. The view from the rear of the houses on the north side of Moray Place is breathtaking. You look out over Lord Moray's pleasure gardens below to the Firth of Forth and the hills of Fife beyond. The light is northern – clear although perhaps a bit cold. The late Lord Cameron – Jock Cameron – lived in one of these houses. One of Scotland's most distinguished judges, he was also a great patron of the arts, a painter and a raconteur – the embodiment, some might say, of Moray Place itself.

Tom and Sybil Gray, RCAHMS SC680456

City of

Literature

Is there something in the Edinburgh water that explains why the city has produced so many writers? BBC Scotland, in a playful mood, broadcast a discussion on this subject some years ago – on the First of April. It is hard to imagine anybody falling for such an absurdity, but the setting of a city – if not its water – probably does help literary creativeness. Edinburgh is a city of fragile beauty, of secretive corners and sudden vistas – such a city will always attract writers and provide them with inspiration.

In the nineteenth century Scotland held the attention of the romantic imagination in all branches of the arts, including music: Mendelsohnn's *Hebrides Overture* and Donizetti's *Lucia di Lammermuir* are examples of Scotland's influence on composers, even if their actual experience of Scotland was slight. Painters, too, were drawn to the magnificence of the Scottish landscape, and indeed often exaggerated it in their romantic enthusiasm: Highland mountains often seem loftier in nineteenth century paintings, waterfalls whiter, mists thicker, and even stags more at bay. Reality may be impressive, but sometimes it is not quite as impressive as we would like it to be.

In literature, the greatest romantic of them all, Walter Scott, put Edinburgh at the heart of European literature, while at the same time effectively inventing an idea of Scotland that proved not only popular but also persistent. The literary critic Stuart Kelly has described that invention in his book *Scottland*: if it had not been for Scott, he suggests, we would never have all the familiar accompaniments of stage Scottishness: the unbiquitous tartans, the shortbread tins with Highland cattle, or even the songs of Harry Lauder and Kenneth McKellar. The point is well made, but even if Scott's vision of his country inspired a raft of romantic contrivances, his literary achievement is still outstanding. Scott is generally credited with the invention of the historical novel. And it was no bad thing for Scotland, surely, that this small nation on the edge of Europe should have produced a writer whose fame was unequalled in his day. It was quite fitting then, that the city should have created for him a monument on such a scale. Most writers would be more than satisfied with a modest plaque on the side of their former home: Scott was given an astonishing spiky edifice, complete with winding stone staircases up which literary pilgrims may climb their way to the top. Dickens did not like this monument; after a visit to Edinburgh he described it as being 'like the spire of a Gothic church taken off and stuck in the ground'. It certainly makes its point: altogether there are over 80 statuettes on its exterior representing characters from Scott's novels or figures from Scottish history. To the modern eye it is, admittedly, odd to the point of being eccentric, but it is a landmark without which one of the best known views of Edinburgh – looking west along Princes Street – would appear very different.

Walter Scott Statue, The Scott Monument, photographed c1875
Sir Walter Scott sits with his faithful deerhound Maida, and a book – presumably one of his own Waverley novels – in his hand. Scott was largely responsible for the prominence of Scotland in the nineteenth century romantic imagination. This statue of white Tuscany marble is at the centre of the writer's extraordinary monument on Princes Street – the largest literary monument in Scotland and probably anywhere else.
Alexander Inglis, Scottish Colorfoto, RCAHMS SC1213919

The story of Edinburgh's association with literature does not begin with Scott, or even with Burns. In the fifteenth and sixteenth centuries the Scottish court was enlivened by a number of poets, or *makars* as they are known in Scots, whose works laid the foundations of a national literature. William Dunbar, a poet, and David Lyndsey, a playwright, both found time outside their courtly duties at Holyrood to satirise the state of Scottish society. Lyndsey was the author of *The Satire of the Three Estates*, which is widely regarded as the first great Scottish play. That tradition of poking fun at human foibles is still strong in Scottish writing, and is probably the reason why Molière translates so well into Scots; more than one modern Scottish writer has produced Scots language versions of the French dramatist's works, with one of these, Liz Lochead's *Tartufe,* proving lastingly popular with the public.

Just about every street of any note in the Old Town has its literary associations. The area around the University is particularly rich in this regard, even if the University's attitude to its architectural heritage has at times been disappointing. The redevelopment of George Square and some of the surrounding streets changed irrevocably an area of great character that could have been conserved and sympathetically modernised. As building after building was replaced, it has become increasingly difficult to find the sites in which men and women of note lived. Plaques that say something like *On this site stood the house in which* … are depressing reminders of how our connections with

our cultural past may be lost, overnight, and so very easily. Cities have to change, of course, but change need not obliterate character and particularity. How dull life will be when we find ourselves all living in cities that look the same as each other – bland, utilitarian boxes of concrete and glass that could be anywhere, and are in fact nowhere.

Buccleuch Place, a wide and airy tenemental street to the south of George Square, survived to an extent the enthusiasms for great expanses of concrete. Number 18 Buccleuch Place is one of the most important addresses in the history of literary Edinburgh, as it was in this house that Francis Horner and Sydney Smith founded the *Edinburgh Review*. This literary journal, first published in 1802, was immensely successful – and highly influential. It attracted contributors from all over Britain and from elsewhere in Europe, including such luminaries as Thomas Carlyle and Walter Scott.

Not far away, in the Greyfriars Kirkyard, may be found the graves of a number of writers including Allan Ramsay, the poet who was also the father of one of Scotland's finest portrait painters; the humanist scholar George Buchanan; and one of the world's most famous bad poets, William McGonagall. Buchanan, who lived in the sixteenth century, was a man of immense erudition and one of the finest Latin stylists of his time. His writings were broad in their scope – history and political philosophy were his strong points, but he wrote verse as well. These writings are comparatively little known today, but Buchanan was nonetheless a man

The Scott Monument, photographed c1890

Here Scott's Monument is the centrepiece of a Victorian pleasure garden. In this view in particular, one can see what the American writer Bill Bryson meant when he described this extraordinary edifice as a 'gothic rocket ship'. Today, it has become such an embedded part of the city that we walk or drive past it and likely do not give it a second thought. If the 'rocket' ever did blast off, the people of the city might pretend, in that particular Edinburgh way, not to notice.
Thomas Polson Lugton, RCAHMS SC466193

Edinburgh is a major character in the Burns story: it is, in a sense, one

of considerable influence. In particular, he was the tutor to James VI and as such played a major role in the education of one of the more literate Scottish kings. But he was a strict tutor, and James's unhappiness may be in part explained by that strictness. Poor James – a lonely young man, starved of affection and surrounded by bickering, suspicion and plots – had his first glimpse of love in the shape of his male cousin, Esmé Stuart. Esmé, who became the Duke of Lennox, was eventually hounded out of Scotland and made to return to France. James wrote a poem on the loss of a colourful and beautiful bird, killed by envy – a phoenix. The phoenix was Esmé.

Kirkyards are nothing if not democratic. Buchanan, the humanist scholar, shares this small patch of earth with an untutored poet whose work never rose above the level of doggerel, but whose memory still survives. William Topaz McGonagall was a native of Dundee, but later moved to Edinburgh, where he lived in College Street just behind the University. He was tormented by the public, who howled with laughter at his appallingly bad verse. But in Edinburgh, for a time at least, he became fairly popular – as a bad poet; he never recognised the problem nor understood why audiences should jeer and throw things at him. His grave in Greyfriars was unmarked, but in 1999 there was erected a stone in his memory, on which, after his name and dates, is inscribed one of his awful verses:

I am your Gracious Majesty
Ever faithful to Thee
William McGonagall, the poor poet
That lives in Dundee.

These lines, drawn from his address to Queen Victoria, are quintessentially McGonagallian. Perhaps his greatest triumph is that which so few writers achieve: an eponymous adjective.

Doggerel can hardly complain about neglect, but the comparative lack of attention paid to the verse of the late eighteenth century poet Robert Fergusson is certainly undeserved. Fergusson died at the age of 24, and his body of work is therefore relatively slender. Its importance, though, is considerable because of its influence on Robert Burns. Reading Fergusson's poetry for the first time creates a strange sense of déjà-vu: this could be from the pen of Burns himself. When Burns came to Edinburgh he was dismayed to find that Fergusson had no gravestone in the Canongate Kirkyard, and he paid for one himself – an act of homage that was movingly referred to in a twentieth century poem by Robert Garioch:

Strang, present dool
Rugs at my hairt. Lichtlie gin ye daur:
Here Robert Burns knelt and kissed the mool.

of his conquests

The grave of Robert Fergusson, Canongate Kirkyard, c1854
This watercolour by the artist James Drummond depicts the grave of the poet Robert Fergusson in the Canongate Kirkyard. Fergusson's work was a major inspiration for Robert Burns, and when Burns came to Edinburgh, he visited this site and was dismayed to discover that there was no monument to the poet. He remedied this at his own expense.
James Drummond, Edinburgh City Libraries, Licensor Scran

These words are very moving. *Here Robert Burns knelt and kissed the mool* – here Robert Burns knelt and kissed the grave-soil. I quoted those lines in one of my own Isabel Dalhousie novels, in which a man facing a momentous event in his life finds himself in the Canongate Kirkyard and remembers Garioch's description of Burns's visit. Garioch's poem seems to capture the feel of that part of Edinburgh so well. It conjures up a strong image of a group of people gathering to honour Fergusson at his grave: gulls wheel against the grey sky, the payers of tribute stand hatless in the *haar* (Edinburgh's special sort of wet fog), and then he, the poet, feels that sorrow, that *dool*, at the thought that Burns himself, in the flush of his Edinburgh fame, should kiss the earth on this humble grave.

The involvement of Robert Burns in Edinburgh began with an unsuccessful visit that failed to attract the sponsorship that he needed. He lodged during that visit in Baxter's Close, which is now part of Lady Stair's Close and the home of the Writers' Museum. His next visit proved more successful – this was the triumph of the rustic poet storming sophisticated Edinburgh society, a story that chimes strongly with our desire to see somebody come from nowhere and get to the top on sheer merit. Edinburgh itself is a major character in the Burns story: it is, in a sense, one of his conquests, taking her place alongside the others who fell for his charms and shared his bed. In that heady love story, Burns not only seduced the drawing rooms of polite society, but revelled in the life of the city's taverns.

Burns in Edinburgh, 1787

This is a picture of a literary lion on safari in Edinburgh. The salon in question was that of the Duchess of Gordon, who is pictured here looking longingly at the poet. Not everyone is paying attention as Burns reads his poem 'Winter Night'. Immediately behind him a man is clearly asleep, and in the background to the left, four figures are enjoying a gossip. Years later, however, even they would no doubt boast of their presence on this occasion and claim to have been entranced by Burns's brilliance.

Goupil, National Museums Scotland, Licensor Scran

Edinburgh has always loved clubs, whether the club is concerned with literature, golf or drink. Burns was introduced to a famous one by the publisher William Smellie. This was the Crochallan Fencibles that met in the Anchor Tavern in Anchor Close. His lively – and extremely earthy – 'unofficial' poetry was inspired by his association with this club. The Crochallan Fencibles would have been disapproved of by the killjoys of the time; today its equivalent would no doubt be similarly viewed by those who take pleasure in stopping others enjoying themselves.

Although Robert Louis Stevenson never attracted quite the universal adoration that Robert Burns enjoys, he remains one of the most well-loved of Edinburgh writers. Stevenson lived at 17 Heriot Row, an address that Andrew Lownie has linked in his extensive study of literary Edinburgh with his heavily autobiographical novel, *The Misadventures of John Nicholson*. Lovers of Stevenson's poetry will recall his 'Leerie the Lamplighter' and will see in this handsome street the very lamps that Leerie lit.

Edinburgh lies at the heart of Stevenson's imagination. Those attuned to the city's sensibility – a subtle thing, as is the sensibility of any place – will *feel* Edinburgh in his writing, even when he is writing about somewhere else. This point is perhaps most frequently made in relation to his enduring tale, *The Strange Case of Dr Jeckyll and Mr Hyde*, thought by many to have been inspired by the story of Deacon Brodie, a respectable burger by day and a thief by night. It may seem strange that we like

to celebrate the occasional criminal – but we do. The Australians love Ned Kelly and devote a whole room in their national art gallery to a set of paintings about the outlaw; the English love Robin Hood; the Americans have a certain affection for Bonnie and Clyde. Deacon Brodie has his own tavern today, at the edge of the Lawnmarket, a popular draw for visitors with a taste for such matters. Stevenson found Brodie interesting enough to write a play about him; perhaps the basis of that interest was the common fascination for the dissonance between outer appearance and inner feeling. A place like Edinburgh, with its aspirations to the genteel and its conceit of itself as an upholder of civilisation and finer values, is a natural setting for this tension. And it comes out at odd times. I remember taking my older daughter to witness the return to Scotland of the Stone of Scone, a Scottish relic removed from Scotland centuries ago and provocatively lodged in London. In a bizarre ceremony intended to assuage Scottish feelings, the Government of the day sent the stone back to Edinburgh, where it was paraded up the High Street on an open army vehicle. The whole occasion was marked by a ceremony in St Giles' High Kirk attended by Scottish notables. The general public, of which my daughter and I were members, stood behind barriers around the edge of Parliament Square, watching as the official guests, many clad in the robes of office, made their way out of the Signet Library towards the Cathedral. There was complete silence (and possibly puzzlement), as befitted an occasion of such peculiar historical significance. And then a man standing beside me shouted out across the square: 'You're nae fooling any of us, ye lackey scum!' It was a heartfelt statement of opposition to the State's attempt to awe the populace with meaningless ceremony, but it was also very funny. Funnier still was the reaction of a well-dressed woman a few yards away who, shocked by the irreverence of the objector, remarked in disapproving tones and in what would be described as a Morningside accent (Morningside being synonymous with genteel respectability): 'Really, one wonders why some people bother to come to these occasions!'

During the twentieth century, literary Edinburgh was affected by the decline of the Scottish publishing industry and the concentration of British publishing in London. The dominance of the new medium of television, with its focus on London and its metropolitan culture, inevitably sapped the sense of Scottishness that had sustained the literary life of Scotland. Few things irritate the citizens of Edinburgh more than to be described as provincial, but that seemed to be the fate awaiting the city and, more generally, Scotland. The Scottish view of the world was, as pointed out by the philosopher George Davie in his important book *The Democratic Intellect*, no longer embraced by its universities, and the things that were distinctive about Scotland were less confident, less well-embedded. But then there came a wave of assertion of Scottish cultural values that was soon to be

The Oxford Bar, Young Street
This is one of the most famous pubs in Edinburgh. It has become a place of modern literary pilgrimage as a result of its being the favourite haunt of Ian Rankin's fictional detective John Rebus.
Chris Robson, Licensor Scran

The 'Banana Flats', Leith, 1982

Although this block of flats is officially called Cables Wynd House, everybody knows them as the 'banana flats', a structure that looks as if it is a team design effort by Le Corbusier and Joseph Stalin. From the 1960s onwards, city planners in Edinburgh and elsewhere thought they were doing people a favour by taking them out of Victorian tenements, such as the ones we see in the background of this picture, and putting them in modern high-rise buildings. Many of these new buildings, both in Edinburgh and Glasgow, have since been dynamited. The 'banana flats' were the home ground of 'Sick Boy', one of the central characters of Irvine Welsh's celebrated novel *Trainspotting*.
RCAHMS SC1141852

Memorial statue, Warriston Cemetery, 2006

It is in this cemetery that one of Ian Rankin's
gruesome fictional murders took place. Ian has
a vivid imagination. This image is the work of the
accomplished American photographer Robert
Reinhard, who has spotted and captured the
particular beauty of many neglected Edinburgh
graveyards and memorials.
Robert Reinhard, RCAHMS DP051606

Gladstone's Land, the Lawnmarket, 1956

Robert Burns' connection with Gladstone's Land is commemorated in the eponymous bar at the centre of the picture. The bar is no longer there, but the two inviting stairways on either side can still be seen. The inscriptions on the windows of the bar tell us that 'Guinness is Good For You' – a claim that contemporary advertising is no longer allowed to make, even if Burns would have enthusiastically supported the sentiment.

Tom and Sybil Gray, RCAHMS SC679851

Lady Stair's House, c1940

First built in 1622, Lady Stair's House, which today is the home of the Writers' Museum, was where Burns lived when he came to Edinburgh. It is claimed that the reason why the stone steps within this house were of uneven height was to serve as an architectural 'burglar alarm'. The unsuspecting burglar would trip on the unexpected stair and thus give away his presence. A modern burglar would, of course, sue the owner.

H D Wylie, RCAHMS SC426602

The Burns Monument, Regent Road, c1836

Robert Burns has been commemorated in more monuments and statues around the world than any other poet in history. This example on Regent Road, overlooking Salisbury Crags and Arthur's Seat, was built in 1830, and is based on an Athenian monument erected by Lysicrates, an enthusiastic patron of music from the fourth century BC. The design is typical of the Greek Style that was adopted in Edinburgh in the late eighteenth and early nineteenth centuries.
W Mossman, RCAHMS, SC932549

Greyfriars Kirkyard, 1912

Once on the fringes of the Old Town, Greyfriars now sits right at the heart of the modern city. The last resting place for many writers and scholars – from Allan Ramsay and George Buchanan to that master of dubious doggerel William McGonagall – it also contains within its sprawling graveyard other important narratives in the history of Edinburgh. At the centre of this photograph is the Martyrs' Monument, a memorial to the Covenanters who were executed for their religious preferences. It is one of the peculiarities of a compact city like Edinburgh that just yards away can be found the mausoleum of Sir George MacKenzie, the King's Advocate, who was chiefly responsible for persecuting the Covenanters. In later years, schoolboys from George Heriot's would play in the graveyard and taunt MacKenzie to rise from his tomb:

'Bluidy MacKenzie, come out if you daur
lift the sneck and draw the bar'

Edinburgh Photographic Society, RCAHMS DP088519

The Scott Monument,
Design Drawing, 1835

If you have never heard of the 'Edinburgh Obelisk' then do not worry – it never existed. Although it could have. The church behind this towering monument is real – St John's, at the corner of Princes Street and Lothian Road. But the obelisk did not go beyond the drawing board. It was part of the competition entry by the architect William Playfair to design an appropriate monument to Walter Scott. Playfair left his mark on Edinburgh in many fine neo-classical exteriors and interiors, but on this occasion he was passed over. As we know, the eventual design would be much stranger, and more distinctive.

William Playfair, RCAHMS DP005114

The Scott Monument,
Contract Drawing, 1841

It is the detail in this extraordinary literary monument that repays attention. Look, for instance, at the narrow winding staircase in this cross-section, drawn by the architect George Meikle Kemp. The monument was inaugurated on 15 August 1846, and built at a cost of £16,000. Kemp, however, never saw it completed – he drowned in March 1844 after falling into the Union Canal. This accident was attributed to his being 'addicted to habits of intemperance'. Whether or not this same 'intemperance' had any bearing on his design is a moot point . . . Certainly, there is a curious and enduring charm in this peculiar product of the Gothic imagination, and visitors still queue to make their way up the cramped stair to the top of tower. One of the hallmarks of a civilisation is that it has things for which there are no conceivable uses. We may never again build something like the Scott Monument, but how fortunate we are that the Victorians built it for us.

George Meikle Kemp, RCAHMS SC466198

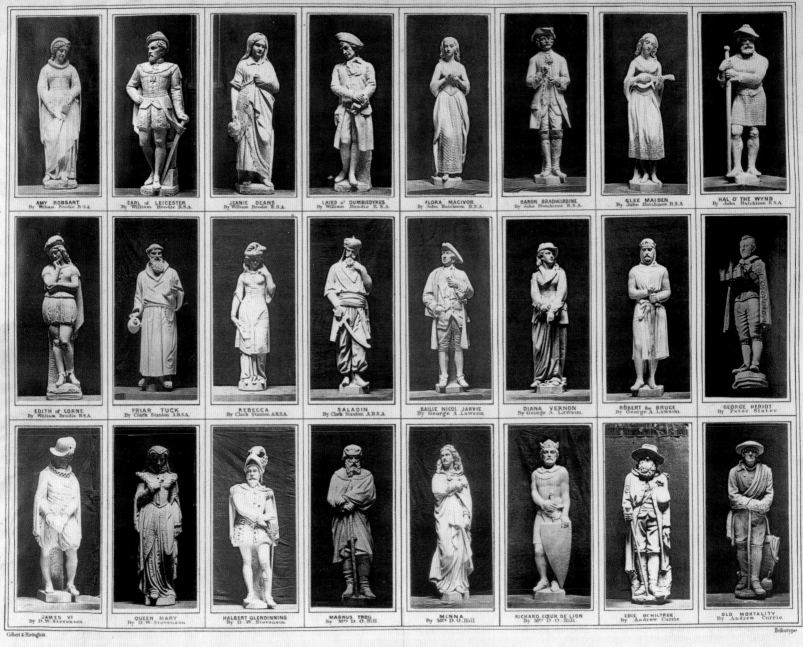

| AMY ROBSART By William Brodie R.S.A. | EARL of LEICESTER By William Brodie R.S.A. | JEANIE DEANS By William Brodie R.S.A. | LAIRD o' DUMBIEDYKES By William Brodie R.S.A. | FLORA MACIVOR By John Hutchison R.S.A. | BARON BRADWARDINE By John Hutchison R.S.A. | GLEE MAIDEN By John Hutchison R.S.A. | HAL O' THE WYND By John Hutchison R.S.A. |

| EDITH of LORNE By William Brodie R.S.A. | FRIAR TUCK By Clark Stanton A.R.S.A. | REBECCA By Clark Stanton A.R.S.A. | SALADIN By Clark Stanton A.R.S.A. | BAILIE NICOL JARVIE By George A. Lawson | DIANA VERNON By George A. Lawson | ROBERT the BRUCE By George A. Lawson | GEORGE HERIOT By Peter Slater |

| JAMES VI By D. W. Stevenson | QUEEN MARY By D. W. Stevenson | HALBERT GLENDINNING By D. W. Stevenson | MAGNUS TROIL By Mrs D. O. Hill | MINNA By Mrs D. O. Hill | RICHARD CŒUR DE LION By Mrs D. O. Hill | EDIE OCHILTREE By Andrew Currie | OLD MORTALITY By Andrew Currie |

Gilbert & Rivington.

Heliotype.

SCOTT MONUMENT, EDINBURGH.

STATUES IN THE NICHES OF THE FOUR MAIN ANGLES.

**Photograph captioned
'Edinburgh at Night', 1907**

This is Robert Louis Stevenson's Edinburgh – a city of mists and mystery. The photograph reveals an Edinburgh of different levels. The road to the right is George IV Bridge, open and rather stately. The road descending to the left is Candlemaker Row which leads down to the Cowgate and the Grassmarket. One is the high road and one is the low road, and this theme of bifurcation and division seems to be written into Edinburgh's DNA. That, at least, is the much-repeated observation about this 'Jekyll and Hyde' city.

Robert Dykes, RCAHMS DP094929.

Images like this continue to act as inspiration. After I first saw this photograph, I began to write a song, which has been set to music by the Scottish composer Tom Cunningham:

Candlemaker Row

In Candlemaker Row October lights
Are individual moons; the sky is dressed
For night; darkness now
Is never far away, days are fleeting
In Candlemaker Row, where the street
Dips so sharply into another world below

In Candlemaker Row, a woman writes
To the husband who is not there,
Grave the task of earning a living
When no living is to be earned;
My Dearest John, Please think of me
In Candlemaker Row, as I think of you

In the distant place where you
Are alone, and far from me;
She signs the note and dates it too
The First of June, nineteen thirty two,
From Candlemaker Row, my dear,
From Candlemaker Row.

View over Princes Street Gardens, 1959

One of the reasons why Edinburgh lends itself to fiction is that it both prompts, and leaves a great deal of work to, the imagination. In the image on the left, we cannot see very much, but we might imagine what is there, or what is about to emerge from the thick fog, possibly only a few feet in front of us. In the photograph on the right, the close is deserted – but is it? The figure framed by the passageway in the distance is either coming or going, and is probably perfectly innocent, but then again . . .

Tom and Sybil Gray, RCAHMS SC681455

Lady Stair's Close, 1959

Tom and Sybil Gray, RCAHMS SC681417

Seat of

Learning

The pictures say it all. The children sit in ordered ranks, each at their desk. Nobody slouches, perhaps because the photographer is present, but one suspects that nobody slouched anyway. In front of the class is the teacher, whose authority is unquestioned and whose pedagogic methods, as likely as not, are severe. There is an awful solemnity to the scene, creating the impression that education in those days was a joyless experience for all concerned. How different from a modern classroom, with its colour and informality; with its air of investigation and its relative freedom. And yet, and yet … there must be moments when today's teachers look back at photographs of these school rooms of the past and sigh. They might be allowed this regret, perhaps, as they battle with behavioural issues, with mobile phones, and with technologically-induced short attention spans.

The sort of classroom pictured in these typical early photographs was to be found in school buildings that are still widely in use in Edinburgh today. Nineteenth century school architecture – solid, functional, and yet not unattractive – can be seen in any Scottish town or city. Great effort was put into the construction of educational buildings in both town and country. These are stone buildings built to last – and they have done just that. The windows are high – what is happening outside has always been a distraction to children, and windows above head-height prevent looking out. There is little ornament, and yet the overall effect is easy on the eye: somehow these buildings just *look like* schools.

I particularly like the surviving separate entrances: above each door one sees, carved in stone, the legend *BOYS* and *GIRLS*. There was no confusion about these matters in those days; even if the doors led into the same classroom. The rough boys would elbow and dig one another in the ribs as they filed through their designated entrance while the girls, inevitably better behaved, would trot quietly through theirs. Perhaps.

The curtilage of the school was dominated by the playground – a bare expanse in which the games of childhood might be played with the minimum props that Victorian children needed to entertain themselves. Today these playgrounds may have the occasional climbing frame for younger children, but they are still essentially rather bare spaces. The small outbuildings that one sees in such schools today were originally the toilet blocks.

The school playground, of course, was not the only place in which children living in the city played their games. Children used to inhabit the streets in a way in which they are no longer allowed to do. The pavements outside a tenement would belong to the children who lived there, and it is on the stone of those pavements that the tribal scrawls of the children would be seen. I remember this vividly: in any residential street one would see squares laid out in coloured chalk for hopscotch. There were blocks and numbers that followed ancient rules handed down

Dean Village, 1947

Every city has its villages. The Dean Village, tucked away below the imposing terraces of the New Town on the banks of the Water of Leith, has retained a very intimate feel. It is one of those places that possesses an atmosphere of timelessness – where children, after escaping from a long day at their school desks, may still run carefree along cobbled streets.

Tom and Sybil Gray, RCAHMS SC679077

from one generation of children to another. They seemed to survive the rain and the feet of passers-by until they faded and sprang up elsewhere. Sometimes they would be accompanied by street art, also made by the children: pictures of stick people or stick children with shocks of hair; pictures of the sun; little lines and squiggles that were perhaps secret maps of an Edinburgh that adults knew nothing about.

Iona and Peter Opie's highly regarded collection of children's folklore drew extensively on the practices of Scottish children, including many in Edinburgh. This marvellous book, *The Language and Lore of Schoolchildren*, takes us a into a world that has now largely vanished – a world in which a children's culture, fashioned and preserved by children themselves, existed alongside the adult world. It was full of sayings and chants; of songs and riddles. It contained what seemed to be a whole world view, and looking now at these old photographs of childhood in Edinburgh, one can almost hear the children's voices as the refrains, admonitory, shocking, or simply nonsensical, echoed about the streets and closes.

But play was one thing – school was quite another. These straightforward local schools were, of course, the expression of an educational ideal that can be traced back to the Scottish Reformation of the sixteenth century and to its insistence that there should be a school in every parish. This is the *fons et origo* of the famed Scottish commitment to education, and it is an objective that lies at the heart of

Scotland's idea of itself. As the country's capital, it is not surprising that Edinburgh should have been at the forefront of Scottish education – and it still is. Today it is a city of schools and universities, many of them with deep roots and a strong sense of their past. As well as being a political and financial hub, Edinburgh is a city that can look any of the great academic centres of the world in the eye.

Many of the schools have an intellectually distinguished history. The Royal High School is the oldest of these, having been founded as a religious institution in 1128. It became the responsibility of the city in the sixteenth century – at that time the school's rector was informed that his responsibility was 'to instruct youth in good manners, piety, doctrine and letters'. The school has migrated around the city. Although currently housed in undistinguished buildings typical of the drab architecture of the second half of the twentieth century, it occupied at one time a particularly fine public building on Regent Road. Prior to that its home was Blackfriars and Infirmary Street, in buildings which now belong to the University. In Infirmary Street these buildings sit cheek by jowl with what used to be the Infirmary Street Baths, which were, a few years ago, transformed into a new home for the Dovecot Tapestry Studios. An old city will always remind us of how the use of buildings will change. Swimming pool into tapestry weaving floor – not exactly a foreseeable progression, but an effective one. But whatever changes of use there may be, there will always be echoes of the building's past life.

A classroom in George Watson's College for Boys, c1915

Educational methods have changed a great deal since these young Watsonians sat their examinations. As this is a fairly early photograph, the subjects would have been told to look diligent and to stay still, so that their features were not blurred by the long exposure times required. Almost all of them obeyed, except for one little boy, just above the master's head, who could not resist the temptation to turn round and sneak a look at the photographer. At this time, George Watson's was housed in a building between Lauriston Place and the Meadows; it did not move to its present location of Colinton Road until the 1930s.

Merchant Company, RCAHMS DP137190

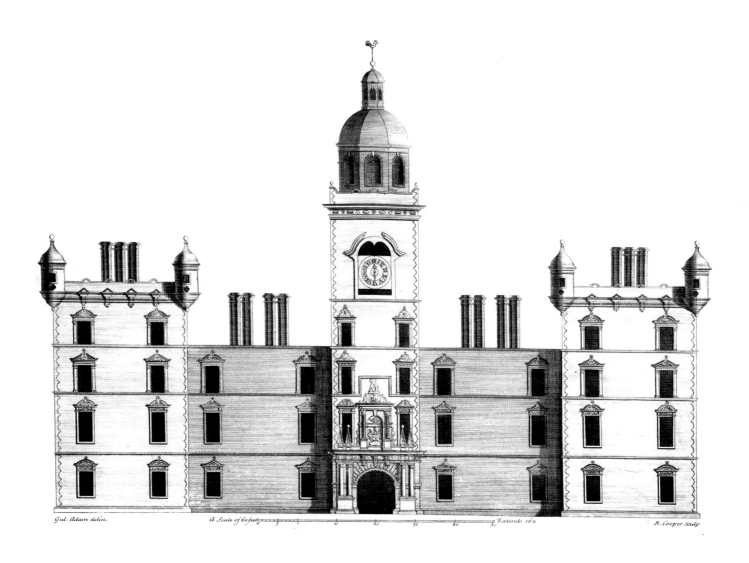

George Heriot's Hospital, c1812

This drawing of the north front of George Heriot's School – or 'Hospital' as it was originally known – is by William Adam, father of Robert Adam, one of Scotland's most famous and successful architects. It is plate 106 of *Vitruvius Scoticus* – a collection of 160 architectural engravings of Scotland's greatest classical buildings, drawn by Adam senior over the course of the first half of the eighteenth century. The engravings were later compiled and published by his grandson – also William – in 1812.
William Adam, RCAHMS SC891864

And that is something that one sees on virtually any walk through the streets of Edinburgh, as buildings reveal their past. At any turn you might find on some facade the outline of an old painted sign – a commercial message, perhaps, that here one might buy pens, or have a suit made, or come in for religious worship. These are like a palimpsest – writings that have been overlaid but may still be revealed and deciphered, reminding us of lives lived in that place, of the concerns of those who have passed their city down to us. A city is simply borrowed by its current inhabitants, possessed for a short time, but inevitably handed on to others. Civic guardians leave their mark, in the shape of street names and monuments, and in the additions and subtractions they make, but their hold on the soul of a city is temporary; the essential character of a city – its spirit of place – is often remarkably tenacious.

Several Edinburgh schools stand out for their sublime buildings. One of these, Heriot's, is housed in the finest creation of seventeenth century Scottish architecture –a building that was to set the aesthetic standard for the design of the New Town. George Heriot, the founder of George Heriot's School, was a Scotsman who made a considerable fortune in London and who left it all for the setting up of a 'hospital' for the 'public weill and ornament of the … burgh of Edinburgh'. The use of the word *ornament* is significant. An ornament, of course, may not be all that ornamental in the modern sense of the word, as long as it is a matter of pride or remark. But the building that was

designed by the royal master-mason, William Wallace, stands out as a real jewel, based on such diverse models as Danish palaces and the plans of the sixteenth century Italian architect Sebastiano Serlio.

Heriot – or *Jingling Geordie*, as he was affectionately known – had been impressed by Christ's Hospital in London, which provided a refuge for orphaned boys. His idea was that his school should give an education to 'fatherless bairns' or to others whose circumstances were difficult. This charitable objective soon caught on, with the setting up of other 'hospitals', such as George Watson's and Daniel Stewart's. The influence of schools such as Watson's has been considerable, and today the professional and commercial life of Edinburgh is extensively populated by Watsonians, as the former pupils of that school are called. In the *Scotland Street* novels Watsonians even become the subject of anthropological interest on the part of one of the characters, Domenica Macdonald, who sees them as a cross between a tribe and a secret society. This is all innocent fun, of course, but Domenica may have a serious point. Every city has its networks, and Edinburgh is no exception. Such networks are often created by people who share common experience – and spending years at school with somebody obviously brings you close together. Those resultant ties can be strong, and may survive into adulthood. In Edinburgh, people know one another in a way which in larger, more impersonal cities they may not. People often assume, as a matter of course, that you know another person about

A city is simply borrowed by its current inhabitants

whom they are talking – and you often do. It can be village-like (as a surprising number of even very large cities may be). Londoners and New Yorkers are often keen to tell you that their cities are composed of villages. When I am in in these large places I find myself surprised to discover that people actually know one another at all – but they do.

With Edinburgh, the whole city seems to be a single large village, rather than many small ones. It is not a city of strangers, and its schools, with their firm idea of their identity, their traditions and history, emphasise deep and lifelong bonds. Does this lead to smugness and parochialism? Is it socially divisive? To an extent this system must do and be all of that, which is regrettable, but the fact remains that these schools make a considerable contribution to education. In recent years, too, they have been increasing their efforts to make more scholarships available, perhaps reviving the objectives of the original Edinburgh 'hospitals' on which they are based. And they have also been obliged, by charity legislation, to ensure that they provide real incidental benefits to the community.

The Merchant Company schools and Heriots have tended to cater for the needs of the Edinburgh middle classes and have been firmly Scottish in their educational philosophy and traditions. Fettes College, by contrast, one of the most striking-looking of the Edinburgh schools, was more modelled on the pattern of English public schools, and even today is predominantly a boarding school that draws its pupils from a wider constituency. The main

school building is an astonishing combination of Scottish Baronial and French Gothic influences – an extravagant unashamed explosion of architectural bravado. I remember on one occasion when I was visiting the school I found myself spending a few minutes waiting in an entrance hall decorated with the portraits of previous masters. A retired member of staff entered the hall and, realising that I was a visitor very courteously explained who was the subject of each portrait. Coming to one now long-deceased master, he pointed to the painting and said, 'Poor fellow! He had no alternative but to drink, you know.' It was a memorable thing to say to a visitor; a moment that Evelyn Waugh might have imagined for *Decline and Fall*. Today Fettes is one of the most highly regarded schools in Britain, turning out well-rounded and highly articulate young people, as well as the occasional prime minister and fictional spy: this is where Ian Fleming had James Bond educated.

The Edinburgh Academy is another school with a strong classical tradition. Sir Walter Scott had a hand in its foundation, and it has produced a large number of distinguished graduates, including the great physicist James Clerk Maxwell, numerous judges of the Court of Session, and countless lawyers. The hall in the main building of the Academy, although of an attractive ovoid design, is not large enough for the closing ceremony of the school year, known as the Exhibition. In recent times, this has been held in St Stephen's Church, a disused Playfair-designed church at the bottom of St Vincent Street. Graduations of any sort always strike me as particularly poignant occasions – they are at one and the same time a sending out into the world and a celebration of achievement, as well as being an occasion of leave-taking, of farewell. The Academy's annual exhibition concludes with a touching ceremony in which the school-leavers individually walk up to shake hands with the Chairman of governing body, then turn round and walk up the aisle, up some steps, and out of the front door into the world. The symbolism is powerful – and moving, as it was for me, when I saw my own daughters take part. Both left school on a sunny morning, and the light flooded in through the door, embracing each pupil as he or she stepped out into their future. Edinburgh is a city that does ceremony well, and the beauty and classical dignity of its streets and buildings add an undeniable gravitas to such events. And why should they not? Ceremonies such as graduations bind us together; remind us of that which we share in life; encourage us to contemplate what it is that we are celebrating, and why we celebrate it.

Fans of the film versions of Ronald Searle's St Trinian's cartoons will be surprised to hear that a school of that name – or close enough – existed in Edinburgh. St Trinean's occupied the large mansion, St Leonard's, that is now in the grounds of the University's Pollock Halls of Residence. This baronial *jeu d'esprit* is today surrounded by contemporary buildings but can hardly fail to be noticed. Searle met some girls from this school during his wartime service and the name so intrigued him that he used it for his fictional creation of the ultimately dreadful girls' school. I had an elderly relative who had been a pupil there. She said that her curriculum vitae was always met with raised eyebrows; nobody would believe that she had actually been to a school called St Trinean's.

The fictional St Trinian's has nothing to do with Edinburgh – apart from owing its name to one of the city's schools. By contrast, another fictional school, Marcia Blaine's, has everything to do with Edinburgh. This was the school at which one of the most memorable characters in Scottish literature taught – Miss Jean Brodie, whose prime was so exquisitely portrayed by the novelist Muriel Spark. Marcia Blaine's does not exist but the model for its heorine is thought to have been one of the teachers at James Gillespie's, the school that Muriel Spark herself attended. A class photograph shows Muriel Spark with her fellow pupils and their teacher. From the photograph she smiles out at us with the look of one who is clearly in her prime.

The University sits at the top of Edinburgh's educational tree. The original *Tounis College*, as the University was known, was granted its royal charter in 1583 by James VI. I have a particular interest in King James, to whom the English language owes such a debt of gratitude. In the scale in which our lives are weighed, his contribution to education and the arts has to be weighed against the relief with which he abandoned his kingdom and moved to London (mind you, looking at the Scotland of his day, who can blame him for that?). There is also the question

'Look at it', he said, 'they call this a place to get an education?'

of his connivance in the torturing of those suspected of witchcraft. (Those matters, of course, cannot be far from one's mind in certain parts of Edinburgh; how many awful public executions did the Old Town witness? How many grim scenes of suffering? In a romantic city it is easy to romanticise a bloody and painful past.) James VI was a child of his time, of course, and he shared the beliefs of his age – something for which we can hardly blame him. If he thought that witches flew around the night sky and could be encouraged to confess by pulling out their fingernails, then just about everybody else at the time shared that belief. Many of the certainties we hold today, may, I suppose, be viewed in the future as bizarre or quaint.

The University's original buildings – three unimpressive courtyards – were on the site of Kirk o'Fields on what was then the edge of the town. Some visitors found it hard to believe that this was a university. James Buchan, the author of an intellectual history of Edinburgh, *Capital of the Mind*, quotes one visitor's description of the college as 'a most miserable musty pile scarce fit for stables'. Oddly enough, four hundred years or so later I had a similar experience as I walked along Chambers Street, beside the present-day Old College. The walls of the Old College at street level are nothing special, and the windows, alas, could do with a bit of a clean. As I walked, I passed a middle-aged couple, whose clothing and demeanour marked them out as visitors from abroad. They were walking slowly and looking up at the Old College. The man then turned to the woman and

said, in a pronounced Australian accent, 'Look at it – and they call this a place to get an education!' They did not appreciate, I think, the reek of history.

Work on the Old College, the dominant building on South Bridge and the seat of the modern University, began at the end of the eighteenth century. It was originally going to be a somewhat complex structure; the end result is more modest in scope than originally planned. And yet, perhaps for that reason, it is one of the finest works of the great architect Robert Adam. Had our critical Australian visitors turned the corner and gone into the Quad through Adam's magnificent entrance with its pillars and domed ceilings they would, I think, have been impressed. After all, there is nothing quite like this in Melbourne or Sydney, much as I admire Melbourne's endless acres of iron-work-adorned Victorian cottages and stand in awe of the view over the harbour to the Sydney Opera House, one of the loveliest buildings human hand has ever made.

The Old College used to house the whole university – science, humanities, and medicine, just as it housed the entire University library. Today the Playfair interiors are used for more limited purposes – for meetings and special lectures on one side, while the Faculty of Law still occupies the other. I have sat through numerous meetings in the University's Raeburn room, a committee room decorated on three sides with Raeburn's portraits of the great professors of his time. They sit looking down on the meeting table and its surrounding chairs, these professors of the late

The New Reading Room of the Playfair Library, University of Edinburgh Old College, 1957

Students sit hard at work in one of the most handsome rooms in the University of Edinburgh. Designed by William Playfair, this was a working library from the early nineteenth century right up until to the 1960s, when the bulk of the University's book collection was moved to new accommodation in George Square. Today, this section of Playfair's interior forms part of the Talbot Rice Gallery – Tom and Sybil Gray, RCAHMS SC680437

eighteenth and early nineteenth centuries, as if bemused by what they hear – and at times they must hear things that test their patience.

But whatever is said in committee rooms would never beat, for sheer oddness, the experience of the mock battles that traditionally surrounded the University's rectorial elections. The office of Rector in an ancient Scottish university is a very particular one: the Rector is the choice of the students and his or her role is to represent the student interest. In Edinburgh the election of the Rector was always accompanied by an extraordinary mock battle in the Old Quad in which opposing factions would defend their corner by throwing things at one another, the missiles fortunately being rotten fruit, flour and the like, rather than anything more serious. The university authorities tolerated this juvenile performance and put up large wooden shutters to protect parts of the building. In the 1970s it suddenly stopped as students realised how childish it was. It was childish, of course, but rectorial battles had long historical roots in the street fights between rival bands of students that were common in the Old Town – students from the University often clashed with boys from the High School, for example, and had to be kept apart at times or violence would occur.

The growth of the University led to its acquiring large swathes of the surrounding Old Town. Impressive new buildings followed this expansion, including the Medical School, built in the late nineteenth century along Italianate lines. I studied Forensic Medicine in this building – two lectures a week – at the feet of one of the old school Edinburgh practitioners of that very particular art: Dr F S Fiddes. The Department of Forensic Medicine had for many years been the domain of the distinguished forensic pathologist Sir Sydney Smith, the author of a set of memoirs called, appropriately enough, *Mostly Murder*. Dr Fiddes was a man of great charm whose modest, restrained manner belied a fervent Scottish patriotism (he was a friend of fiery nationalists, such as Wendy Wood).

Dr Fiddes very gently introduced his law students to the exhibits in the glass cases. A strong stomach was helpful. This, he said, is an oesophagus of a man who swallowed his pipe … This is what a knife will do … We glanced, but then looked away again quickly, shuddering; that could be any one of us. We looked out of the window, to the roofs on the other side of Bristo Place; stone crenulations incised against the sky. Dr Fiddes dictated his notes and we wrote down his words. *Cause of death … asphyxiation … blunt instruments … fracture of the skull … post-mortem examination revealed …*

Behind the Medical School, towards the Meadows, is George Square, changed profoundly in the 1960s by the erection of modern structures which, as the *Buildings of Scotland Edinburgh* volume tersely points out, pay no attention to one another or to the Georgian survivors. The remaining small Georgian houses became for the most part university departments, and still are. Until very

A rectorial battle in the Old College Quad, 1959
This is not an image of revolutionary conflict. What appears to be tear gas is, in fact, flour. Students are more mature these days.
The *Scotsman*, Licensor Scran

recently, Edinburgh University Press occupied one of them – a bustle of creativity shoe-horned into offices that would once have been the living and sleeping quarters of families. So many offices in the older parts of Edinburgh are just that – ingeniously recycled domestic space. It was in one of these offices that I slipped across the desk of an editor the manuscript that was to begin the No 1 Ladies' Detective Agency series and said: 'This is about a woman in Botswana who sets up a small detective agency'. And the editor on the other side of the desk simply said, 'I see'.

The University of Edinburgh may be the biggest university in the city but it is not the only one. Heriot-Watt University has now decamped to the outskirts, but it once occupied much of one side of Chambers Street, opposite the Museum. Then there is Edinburgh Napier University, which grew up around the old castle of

Sir John Napier, incorporating its ruins in a modern building on Colinton Road, near Holy Corner (so-called because of its four churches all within a few yards of one another). Queen Margaret University has been more peripatetic then the others: it stemmed from that great institution, the domestic science college in Atholl Crescent, moved out to sylvan surroundings beyond the zoo, and then further east into sparkling new buildings in the old coal-mining belt near Newcraighall.

Gaudeamus igitur. So Let Us Rejoice. The student life today is probably a bit more sober, a bit more care-laden than it was a few decades ago. But the advice of the Gaudeamus is surely correct. There will be plenty of time in the future to contemplate the harsh reality of life – student days in Edinburgh should reflect the romance, the mystery and all the light-hearted possibilities that this beguiling city can inspire.

Lindsay Stewart Lecture Theatre, Napier University, 2007
Edinburgh has some interesting examples of adventurous architecture – and this building, designed by BDP architects, is as adventurous as the city gets. It also provides a very useful educational space that takes maximum advantage of natural light. Napier is one of the newer universities in the city, and its innovative approach to education has proved very successful – RCAHMS DP03044

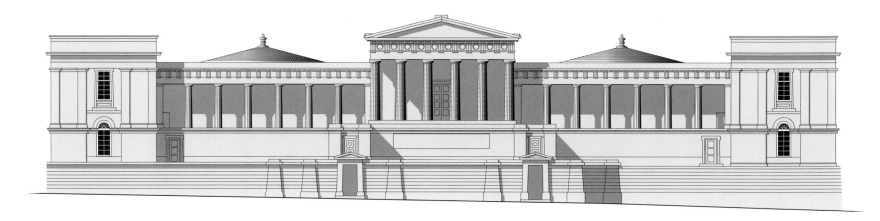

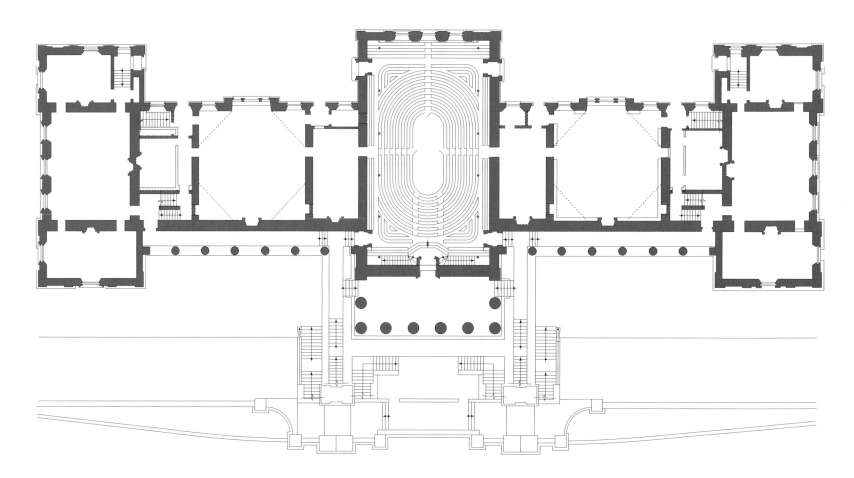

The Old Royal High School, Regent Road, 2004

This august building reflects the grandeur of the city's ambitions for the area around Calton Hill. The school itself, along with its pupils, vacated this impressive neo-classical 'temple' many years ago, and ever since there has been a great deal of discussion as to appropriate uses for it. When plans were being laid for a new Scottish Parliament, the option of using the High School was favoured by some. Of course, as we know, the decision was taken to build something very different in the valley below. As this survey drawing neatly shows, one of the School's most notable interior features was its great Debating Chamber, with its ordered rows of oval seating.
RCAHMS GV005420

**The Old Royal High School with
the Burns Monument in the distance, 1895**

Henry Bedford Lemere, RCAHMS SC683128

The Old Royal High School, 1895

Henry Bedford Lemere, RCAHMS SC683126

The main portico of the Old Royal High School, c1940

B C Clayton, RCAHMS SC1122089

The Old Royal High School, c1940

B C Clayton, RCAHMS SC1122090

left

Canongate Kirkyard looking up to the Old Royal High School, c1930

Francis Caird Inglis, RCAHMS SCI223111

above

The Old Royal High School, c1820

This painting shows what the nineteenth century worthies of the city wanted the 'Athens of the North' to look like. The buildings appear considerably cleaner and more glowing than they are in real life. This was a romantic moment in Scotland's existence. Many paintings of the time deliberately made the nation's landscape look more impressive than it actually was. The Highlands, for example, were depicted as a wilderness of steep mountains that had mysteriously been elevated by several thousand feet. The Royal High School was designed in concert with its surrounding landscape – and in particular the National Monument, which was being built simultaneously on Calton Hill above. The lofty aim was to create an 'Edinburgh Acropolis'.

The Royal Scottish Academy, RCAHMS SCI013507

George Heriot's Hospital, c1690

This view of the charity school for 'puir fatherless bairns' was drawn in the seventeenth century by the engraver John Slezer for his landmark book of Scottish buildings and landscapes, *Theatrum Scotiae*. Interestingly, as the late professor of architecture Charles McKean noted, the school's role as a place for orphans was even reflected in its architecture – the frontage of the building was designed in a style known rather colourfully as Dorico Bastardo. When first built, the entrance was topped by a spire, which later became the building's distinctive clocktower. At the time of this engraving, Heriot's was surrounded by substantial open grounds. In the fields in the right foreground, we see four children escaping . . .
John Slezer, RCAHMS SC756206

Statue of George Heriot in the quadrangle of George Heriot's School, c1920

George Heriot, who was James VI's goldsmith, is immortalised in stone above an archway leading out of the north side of the school's quadrangle. Peering round the columns below him are the blurred faces of inquisitive boys.
Francis M Chrystal, RCAHMS SC1132986

DANIEL STEWART'S COLLEGE, EDINBURGH. NORTH FRONT. 507.

Edinburgh Schools

The architecture of Scottish schools was nothing if not distinctive – solid, functional, although sometimes with flourishes of ornament. These buildings speak of purpose and of rigour – although perhaps rather less of joy. We should not be surprised: Scotland has always taken education very seriously.

clockwise from top left
Bruntsfield Primary School, c1900
Henry Bedford Lemere, RCAHMS SC680362

Fettes College, c1915
Francis M Chrystal, RCAHMS SC109283

Daniel Stewart's College for Boys, c1870
Alexander Inglis, RCAHMS DP075264

Mary Erskine School, Queen Street, c1900
Merchant Company, RCAHMS DP137241

James Gillespie's Hospital, Gillespie Crescent, 1880
Alexander Inglis, RCAHMS SC1235387

George Watsons' College for Boys, Lauriston Place, c1915
Merchant Company, RCAHMS DP137187

above
Classroom, Daniel Stewart's College for Boys, c1900
A class of small boys, presumably singing. Few of them look enthusiastic. Some hide behind their books. Look at their boots: solid, heavy and laced up beyond the ankle, they were unlikely to have been comfortable. At least they were shod, however – many children of the time had no shoes at all. In rural schools in Scotland at this time, some children walked barefoot to school over several miles.
Merchant Company, RCAHMS DP137216

Edinburgh Merchant Company School Gymnasium, c1910

All that is known of this photograph is that it was taken during the Edwardian period, and the school shown was run by the Edinburgh Merchant Company. Note that even the most ridiculous poses are held in a ladylike manner. Jean Brodie would have recognised this, and approved.
Merchant Company, RCAHMS SC1110222

This image is of such bizarre composition that it provokes much speculation in the viewer – or at least it does for me. Here is my response, in a song which has been set to music by the composer Tom Cunningham:

The Gym Lesson
Under the watchful eye of Miss Mackay
Who's quite immune to every sigh
And claim of tiredness, or sore knees,
Whose eagle vision always sees
What's going on behind her back,
Who knows what effort lazy girls will lack –
That's Miss Mackay, of Gym,
That's Miss Mackay, of Gym.

A growing girl, says Miss Mackay,
May not appreciate how and why
Physical effort is required,
She's unlikely to be inspired
By exercise, but we who care
Know what benefit awaits her there,
Says Miss Mackay, of Gym,
Says Miss Mackay, of Gym.

And for each girl there did await
A different and distinctive fate:
Marjory Macpherson, on the right,
Became a lady of the night,
While Ethel Parker on the ropes
Succeeded with artistic hopes;
And Kirsty Snodgrass, hands on head,
Crashed her aeroplane and is now dead;
It goes to show, said Miss Mackay,
It goes to show, said Miss Mackay.

And Miss Mackay herself is gone,
She fought a battle others won,
She made girls fit, but she herself
Was awfully careless with her health;
She liked to smoke and also drank,
And so her lungs both slowly shrank,
And people watched and said, 'Oh Jings!
She was a Highlander and they like such things.'
But we shall miss you, Miss Mackay,
But we shall miss you, Miss Mackay.

Edinburgh Merchant Schools, Home Economics class, c1910

A hundred years ago, girls and boys would enter schools by separate entrances – if they even shared the same schools at all. The curriculum for the sexes was also very different. Thankfully, much has been done to remove that gender bias today. Now boys are taught the domestic science being demonstrated in the photograph on the left and girls can enjoy the woodwork being done by the boys on the right.

Merchant Company, RCAHMS SC1110215

**Edinburgh Merchant Schools,
Woodwork class, c1910**
Merchant Company, RCAHMS SC110216

India Place, Stockbridge, 1960

This is one of the streets in the north of Edinburgh that fell foul of the 1960s enthusiasm for clearance: today, it no longer exists. Had these streets been better cared for the buildings would have provided many more years of service and the flats we see here would by now be highly desirable dwellings for young IT professionals. Their scale was human. Children populated the streets then. The pavement was their territory; they drew upon it and they played their games on it. These two boys in the foreground have a go-kart almost identical to the one I had as a boy. Their steering system is the same – a rope tied to each end of the front axle. The car parked behind them was probably not much more mechanically sophisticated.
The *Scotsman*, Licensor Scran

East Princes Street Gardens, 1968

Children have always possessed sometimes real, sometimes imagined maps of cities that adults do not know and cannot see. They would know the best places to play – where to kick a football or enjoy a game of hide and seek. Or, as in this image, where to commune with the city's avian population. With the classical columns of the Royal Scottish Academy in the background, two little girls are well received by the pigeons of Princes Street Gardens.

Newsquest, Licensor Scran

next pages

The Flodden Tower in the Vennel, and St John's Close in the Canongate, c1915

Young boys and girls are captured here in the narrow spaces of the Old Town. There is a social gulf between the children in these two pictures. The boys on the left have a much better chance in life than the children on the right, standing in their doorway in the Canongate. For all the much-vaunted egalitarianism of Scotland, there have always been stark inequalities, as these photographs, taken in the same period, demonstrate. The desire to attend to this situation is strong in Scottish political culture.

Francis M Chrystal, RCAHMS SC1100947 and SC556284

left

**The Playfair Library, The University
of Edinburgh Old College, c1900**

This was the main university library until its
replacement (pictured right) was built in George
Square in the 1960s to a design by Sir Basil
Spence. The Playfair Library still has books in
its book bays, but they are never read today.
Instead, this room is used for formal occasions –
receptions and conferences. It is lined with busts
of former professors of the university, rather
lonely now in the absence of students.
Scottish Colorfoto, RCAHMS SC1076495

above

**The University of Edinburgh George
Square Library, 1968**

Henk Snoek, Sir Basil Spence Archive,
RCAHMS SC1030953

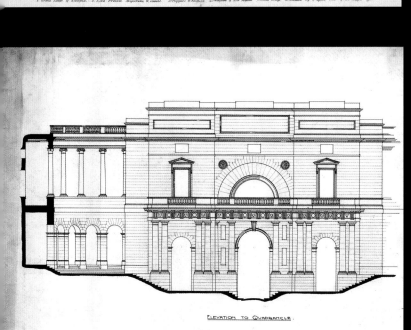

ELEVATION TO QUADRANGLE.

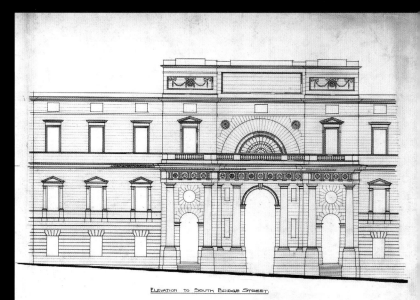

ELEVATION TO SOUTH BRIDGE STREET.

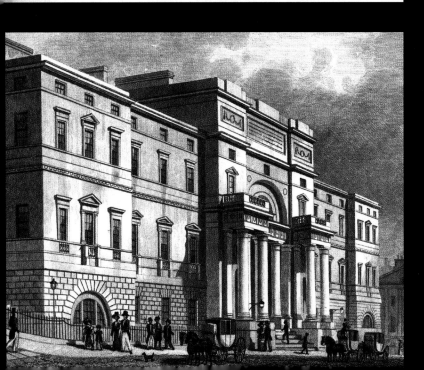

The Ceremony of Laying the Foundation Stone of the NEW COLLEGE of EDINBURGH & November 16, 1789.

Edinburgh University Old College

The Old College – which was, of course, originally the 'New' College – had a complex architectural history and was initially going to be much larger than it eventually turned out. The buildings once housed many of the University's departments, but now only the School of Law remains. The quad at the centre was used for a long time as a car park, but has recently been rehabilitated and is an impressive place once again. I worked in this building for many years and occupied a number of different offices on its north side. When I used to leave the building I always looked up at the figure standing on top of the tower – a gilded statue we knew as the golden boy. Immediately opposite the entrance was the city's oldest bookshop, James Thin. The Thins had been booksellers, printers and publishers for generations and I had dealings with the last generation of the family to be involved in the business. The store is now run by Blackwell's, the Oxford booksellers, but many people in Edinburgh still think of it as Thin's.

top left
The Ceremony of the Laying of the Foundation Stone of the New College of Edinburgh, November 16 1789
Richard Emerson, RCAHMS SC1233386

The Old College looking along the South Bridge, c1915
Francis M Chrystal, RCAHMS SC1098280

middle left
Elevations showing Robert Adam's design for the entrance block for the Old College, drawn 1906
J B Lawson, RCAHMS DP011927

bottom left
Engravings showing the Old College before the construction of its dome, c1819
J H Storer and Thomas H Shepherd, RCAHMS SC465067 and SC465083

right
The University of Edinburgh Old College, South Bridge, c1900 and c1920
Francis Caird Inglis, Scottish Colorfoto, RCAHMS SC1119786 and SC1240975

The University of Edinburgh
Medical School, c1890
The entrance to the medical school – note the
Florentine arches. Once inside one could be in Italy.
In my days as a student, the Department of Forensic
Medicine was immediately off to the left after the gate.
Alexander Inglis, RCAHMS SC1235432

McEwan Hall, Teviot Place, c1900
This has been the scene, for over a century, of numerous
university graduations. The organ is played before the
ceremony and students then mount the steps and face their
professors seated in three rows of seats. The graduation
involves being briefly capped by the principal with a cap made,
tradition holds, from a piece of John Knox's breeches.
Alexander Inglis, RCAHMS SC1200655

West side of George Square, c1950
Rather little of the original George Square survives. Its destruction was lamentable but at least we have this stretch of the original buildings on the west side to remind us of just how charming it once was. This used to be the home of Edinburgh University Press, and it was through one of these doors that I walked – with some trepidation – to submit the manuscript of my first novel, *The No.1 Ladies Detective Agency*.
National Museums Scotland, Licensor Scran

David Hume Tower, George Square, 1965
The *Scotsman*, Licensor Scran

Working

Lives

Henry Cockburn, one of my favourite Edinburgh figures,

was a lawyer – eventually a judge of the Court of Session – author and a witty observer of the city's people and their ways. He was also an exponent of architectural conservation: the body that has, more than any other, fought to preserve Edinburgh from the depredations of developers, *The Cockburn Association*, is named in his honour. This is Cockburn writing in the early nineteenth century about the city's fish market, something that he probably had no wish to preserve:

> The fish were generally thrown out in the street at the head of the close, whence they were dragged by dirty boys or dirtier women, and then sold unwashed – for there was a not a drop of water in the place – from old, rickety, scaly, wooden tables, exposed to all the rain, dust and filth; an abomination the recollection of which greatly impaired the pleasantness of the fish at a later hour of the day.

And if that is not enough to put one off, then here he is on the vegetable markets:

They were entirely in the hands of a college of gin-drinking women, who congregated with stools and tables round the Tron Church. A few of the aristocracy of these ladies – the burgo-mistresses, who had established a superior business – the heads of old booths – marked their dignity by an awning of dirty canvas or tattered carpet ... Fruit had a place on the table, but kitchen vegetables lay bruised on the ground.

These insalubrious, bustling markets were a source of other dangers and not just of germs. A report in the *Caledonian Mercury* in 1800 refers to a gang of female pickpockets operating in the Fish Market – the newspaper observing that the gang had recently arrived from Glasgow. And in the Fleshmarket, which occupied the ground on which the Scotsman Building was later constructed, the Council is recorded as having had difficulties with packs of aggressive dogs owned by the butchers and their servants; the city fathers saw no reason why a butcher should have as many as seven or eight dogs. One can imagine the stench, and the noise of the Old Town: the barking of dogs, the squealing of animals, the cries of the traders, the clatter of carts bringing produce to the various markets.

Specialised markets existed in various parts of the city. In 1840 there were ten of these including grain and associated products in the Grassmarket, where cattle and horse dealers also operated. The fish market used to be in Old Fishmarket

Old trams against the backdrop of Edinburgh Castle, 1950
The junction of Princes Street and Frederick Street is captured here in the earlier days of the Edinburgh trams. People are making their way to work on what looks like a rather cold and misty morning.
Tom and Sybil Gray, RCAHMS SC679146

Close, described by Cockburn as a 'steep, narrow, stinking ravine'. Later it moved to the area that is now occupied by Waverley Station. The old Waverley Market had a roof put on it in 1874 and it continued to be a useful public space until it was converted into the Princes Mall – a collection of modern shops. Today the markets have disappeared – the end of a long process whereby individual shops took over the role that markets played. Is our life the poorer for the loss of markets? Of course it is. Buying produce and other necessities in a market is a totally different experience from doing the same thing in shops. Marketplaces are social spaces in which people parade, converse and observe the business of others. Market transactions are more personal, and allow for comparison of wares, bargaining and banter. Only the odd 'pop-up' Farmers' Market exists to remind us of what has been lost. One is held on Saturdays, on the roof of a multi-storey carpark under the towering Castle Rock. The same people go there every week, friends meet and chat over cups of coffee from coffee stalls, musicians play, and there is a strong sense of sharing in an activity with others. It could not be a more different experience from pushing a trolley down the aisles of a supermarket stocked with neatly packaged foodstuffs. Of course, the process of buying and selling is probably going to become more depersonalised yet. Online shopping may be convenient, but it is already beginning to take its toll on bricks and mortar shops. What would happen to our city streets if the small shops that give them character and life were to be driven out of business by the behemoths of the internet?

That has not happened yet, and may not. However convenient online purchase may be, people still want the experience of seeing and handling the things they buy. As a result, there will still be shops, although they will undoubtedly find life more difficult. Small shops are probably destined to become more specialised, leaving prosaic shopping, including most groceries, to malls and out-of-town shopping centres. In this respect, Edinburgh is fortunate in having plenty of interesting smaller shops in places like Victoria Street, with its print sellers, outfitters and jewellers, or Dundas Street with its galleries and antique shops. Dundas Street is very much frequented by the characters in my novels, both the Isabel Dalhousie series and the Scotland Street novels. Isabel sits in the window table of Glass and Thompson's bistro, where she meets her friends and watches the passing life of the city. A few paces down Dundas Street brings her to the Scottish Gallery, which is run by Guy Peploe, the grandson of the great Scottish colourist Samuel Peploe. Guy appears in the books – as himself – along with many other real people. With Isabel he discusses Scottish art, one of her strongest interests – after philosophy, of course. Dundas Street is also the setting of the fictional café run by Big Lou in the Scotland Street series – a useful backdrop for the various characters in those books to talk about their day-to-day concerns, before going off to the real Valvona and Crolla, an Edinburgh institution at the top of Leith Walk. Valvona and Crolla is run by an enthusiastic couple who themselves

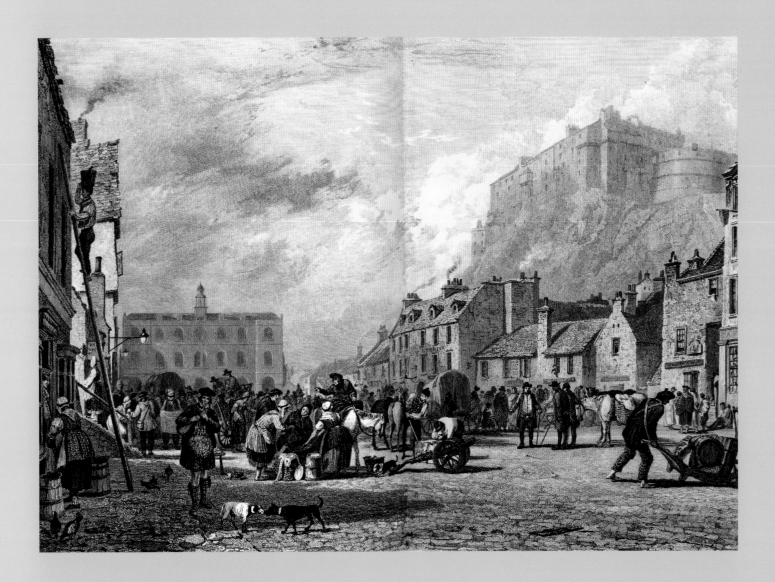

The Grassmarket, 1820

Against the solid bulk of the Castle, the rickety nature of the buildings in the Grassmarket stands out – many of these would be knocked down and rebuilt during the Victorian era. In Edinburgh, businesses and dwellings rubbed shoulders in a very intimate way. Shops would also be homes for numerous people. The tradition of having small workshops in residential areas has persisted for centuries, and this gives a strong lived-in and worked-in feel to many parts of the city.

A W Calcott, RCAHMS DP094885

appear in the books – Philip and Mary Contini. For two generations their families have brought the delights of the Italian table to the people of this city, and Mary has written a moving book, *Dear Francesca*, which is addressed to her daughter. Although ostensibly a recipe book, it is much more than that, being an exploration of Italian heritage and the links, culinary and otherwise, between Italy and Scotland. And those links have been rich and productive: Richard Demarco, an artist and gallery owner renowned for his intense love of the city and its architecture, is one of many people of Scottish-Italian descent who have left a positive stamp on Edinburgh, bringing Italian artistic passion and flair to the normally somewhat cautious Scottish soul.

And of course in almost all of my Edinburgh novels the characters inevitably at some stage make their way to Jenner's, that great Edinburgh store which dominates one end of Princes Street. Jenner's has always represented Edinburgh – or at least a certain part of Edinburgh – distilled. Edinburgh primness and respectability is, of course, a huge joke that we all enjoy. Jenner's, with the grandeur of its building, and its tea room, is the very embodiment of the old-fashioned city – its face turned firmly away from any form of coarseness or vulgarity. Of course life, for most, is distinctly not a matter of cream teas and perjink respectability, but it adds to the texture and variety of a city to have such things in our midst. (Perjink, incidentally, is a Scots word that I

think Edinburgh should claim for itself. Perjink is neat and tidy, perhaps a bit fussy. And it is the fussiness that makes it a real Edinburgh word. Edinburgh is not at all fantoosh – another wonderful Scots word. Other cities can be fantoosh (flashy and showy), but not Edinburgh. If you want to buy anything really fantoosh, you probably have to go somewhere other than Jenner's.

There used to be other great department stores, with large, impressive buildings even if they were not as grand as Jenner's. R & W Forsyth was one. It was on Princes Street, near Jenner's, and it was an outfitters 'home and colonial' (how many young men bought lightweight tropical suits there prior to going off to Hong Kong to work for Jardine Mathieson or to spend humid years in Singapore or Penang?). Patrick Thompson's was on the Bridges, opposite the Scotsman building, and there was J & R Allen's on the corner of Chambers Street. Allen's had a magnificent system for taking the money – a network of tubes into which a large cartridge containing the cash tendered and the invoice were sent whooshing away pneumatically to some distant cash room, returning later with the change. Both of these stores have gone, as has Goldberg's in Tollcross, a building of breath-taking 1960s ugliness, now fortunately no more. Had it not been demolished, it would have been high on the list of demolitions to which we might look forward. The leading candidate on the current list is the monstrosity in Lady Lawson Street – the mistake in concrete – a joyless

Jenner's Tea Room, 1895

This is the headquarters of genteel Edinburgh. Imagine the conversations that have taken place under this particular ceiling over the past one hundred years or so: the gossip, the polite – or not so polite – put-downs, the looks of disapproval. Jenner's features in a number of the Scotland Street novels – not least as a place where the characters go while the author is deciding what should happen next – Henry Bedford Lemere, RCAHMS SC678376

I remember the wind that used to blow, at gale force it seemed,

building in the same Eastern European style that also inspired the St James Centre at the end of Princes Street. Auden was very astute when he said that the trouble with concrete is that it de-sexes the space it occupies . . .

Demolition was the rallying cry in respect of a famous piece of sculpture that once presided over the middle of the traffic circle outside St Mary's Cathedral. Many will still remember it, but few, I'm afraid, will regret it. It was a curious metal tower, rather like one of scaffolding erected by a drunken workman, along the struts of which fluorescent light strips had been added. These changed colour with the wind. It was very ugly and inappropriate for its surroundings, and a witty campaign was mounted for its dismantling.

Architecture – both its grand exclamations, and also its little grammatical necessities – has always been important to Edinburgh. Passageways, street corners and staircases that link one place to another are as significant to the character of the city as grand civic buildings and sculptures. One of my first memories of Edinburgh, for instance, is of walking up the steps that led from Waverley Station to Princes Street. I remember the wind that used to blow, at gale force, it seemed, up from the station below, with its great glass roof and its characteristic station smell. I remember the army surplus shop that used to be half way down the steps on the left, selling heavy green jackets and boots and tam o'shanters. I think one passed a lift that led from the steps into the North British Hotel. (I still

call it the 'NB' even if it now rejoices under the name of the Balmoral Hotel. Today nobody could call anything North British because of the associations of that term with the denial of Scotland. Scotland may be in the north of Britain, but it is definitely not North Britain.)

The North British Hotel is immortalised in an amusing poem by Robert Garioch, *Glisk o' the Great*. The poet speaks in the voice of a bystander seeing prominent citizens coming out of the NB Grill and getting into what he describes as a 'muckle great municipal Rolls Royce'. Now that, he says, is quite a sight, and although you and I cannot join in, 'it gives our toon some tone, you'll all agree'. Garioch had a good eye: he understood the pomposity and self-importance of local politicians and caught very acutely the whiff of slightly pained dignity that has always drifted around Edinburgh. Glasgow people would know what he meant, as they have always playfully – and lovingly, too – hinted that Edinburgh has a particularly good conceit of itself. If Glasgow is the jovial uncle who enjoys a drink and has a twinkle in his eye, then Edinburgh is the slightly detached maiden aunt. So the popular images would have it, but nobody takes these seriously – or not *entirely* seriously. On the subject of the rivalry of the two cities, I cannot resist telling the story of a friend of mine who took his then six-year-old daughter on her first trip to Glasgow on the train from Waverley Station. They pulled into Queen Street Station at the end of the journey and stepped out onto the platform. It was at

up from the station below

this point that the young girl asked, in a very loud voice and to the considerable embarrassment of her father, 'What's that smell?' This story would be appreciated, I think, by Glasgow people who would say that it says something about Edinburgh rather than Glasgow.

The train to Glasgow snakes out of Waverley Station and disappears a minute or two later into a tunnel under the National Gallery of Scotland. In one of the Scotland Street novels, Bertie Pollock, a six-year-old boy who is much oppressed by his mother, makes his break for freedom with his friend, Ranald Braveheart Macpherson. The two boys buy train tickets to Glasgow but do not complete the journey, as they get off the train at Haymarket Station, a mile or so down the track, believing that it is Queen Street Station in Glasgow. Bertie is destined to be unsuccessful in his search to escape the baneful influence of his mother; Glasgow is for him a promised land – a place where he will be able to lead the life of an ordinary boy, owning a Swiss Army penknife and eating the unhealthy foods that his mother denies him.

There is another railway tunnel running north from Waverley Station which is now bricked in at the station end but which remains intact. This is the Scotland Street tunnel, along which the Edinburgh, Leith and Newhaven Railway – later the Edinburgh, Leith and Granton Railway – used to run. This tunnel was built in 1847 to link Canonmills with what was then called the Canal Street Station – a station that was later incorporated into Waverley

Advert for the North British Hotel, 1905
Impeccably dressed Edinburgh Edwardians promenade past the 'North British' Hotel – better known today as the Balmoral.
Scotland's Industrial Souvenir, RCAHMS DP144394

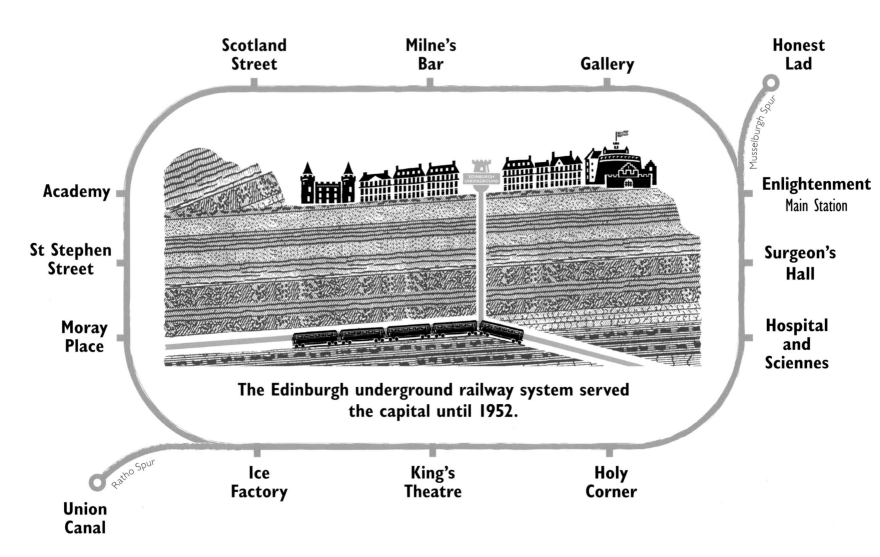

Scotland Street

Milne's Bar

Gallery

Honest Lad

Academy

Enlightenment Main Station

St Stephen Street

Surgeon's Hall

Moray Place

Hospital and Sciennes

Musselburgh Spur

The Edinburgh underground railway system served the capital until 1952.

Ratho Spur

Ice Factory

King's Theatre

Holy Corner

Union Canal

The Edinburgh Underground, 2011

On 1 April 2011, I wrote a playful story, printed in the *Scotsman* newspaper, about Edinburgh's lost underground network. It was a nostalgic history of something that never existed. Here, the illustrator Iain McIntosh imagines a design for the underground station map.

Iain McIntosh

Station. The ultimate destination was Granton Harbour, allowing people to travel by rail from the city centre to Granton and from there by ferry over to Fife. From 1850 a train ferry carried the railway carriages across the Firth of Forth, thus linking Edinburgh with cities such as Perth and Dundee. That was before the construction of the iconic Forth Railway Bridge in 1890.

The Scotland Street tunnel is a considerable engineering achievement. It runs just a few feet beneath Scotland Street but is almost 50 feet below street level by the time it reaches St Andrew's Square. The trains were drawn up and down the line by a rope pulled by a static engine. When the line to Granton was connected to the main railway line in the east of the city, the rationale for the tunnel disappeared and thereafter it was used for a range of different purposes, including the cultivation of mushrooms, the storage of cars, and as an air-raid shelter. Today one can still peer into the tunnel at its Scotland Street end: the air is dry and cool – the characteristic breath of a tunnel.

Subterranean tunnels through the heart of a city are a gift to a novelist. The Scotland Street tunnel makes an appearance in the Scotland Street books when one of the characters leads an expedition up it in the direction of Waverley Station. To their surprise they discover another tunnel – this time a fictional one – branching off under Princes Street. This tunnel comes up under the floor of the New Club, and the small band of surprised explorers find themselves looking up through the floorboards at the annual general meeting of the Edinburgh establishment. Absurd, of course, but the idea of there being an establishment that meets to discuss strategy is exactly the sort of thing that real establishments always deny.

A few years ago, on April First, I wrote about another fictional Edinburgh tunnel – or rather series of tunnels. It was a history and a lament for the demise of the Edinburgh Underground. The *Scotsman* made a two-page feature of it and it succeeded in hoodwinking a considerable number of people. I received letters from those who expressed an interest in visiting some of the stations and asking whether access was allowed. The stations never existed, but if Edinburgh had ever had an underground system, then surely stations rather like this *might* have existed:

The Edinburgh Underground consisted of a central, circular route with two spurs going off to the east (the Musselburgh Spur) and west (the Ratho Spur). The final stations on each of these branches were *Honest Lad* and *Union Canal*. During the Edinburgh trades holidays, it was possible to buy a cheap ticket for one-and-twopence that would take an entire family to either of these termini for a picnic or other outing. The inner circle started and ended at the system's main station, *Enlightenment*, which was on the High Street, not far from the Mercat Cross. The name of this station derived from the famous remark on the number of men of genius in the Scottish Enlightenment whose hand could be shaken if one stood at that spot for an hour or two. *Enlightenment* was not only the principal station; it was the most beautifully decorated, latterly with a remarkable set of murals by Phoebe Anna Traquair depicting the development of political economy and the notion of moral sympathy in the writings of Adam Smith and David Hume. From *Enlightenment* the line dipped sharply down to *Gallery*. As the name suggested, this station, reached from the foot of the Playfair Steps, catered for those who wished to visit the National Gallery of Scotland or the Royal Scottish Academy. Academicians of the RSA were, in fact, entitled to travel free, provided that they boarded at this station, although latterly many of them abstained from taking advantage of this privilege.

And the essay ended with this, I hoped, giveaway:

That was the Edinburgh underground, and those were its stations. Sometimes, when I walk across the Meadows, I pause and close my eyes; and imagine for a moment that I hear, down beneath my feet, the passing rumble of an underground train – which is strange, perhaps, as no trains went that way.

Edinburgh has never been viewed as an industrial city in the sense in which Glasgow has, but it would be a mistake to think that it was never a manufacturing centre: it was. While Edinburgh lacked the heavy industry that developed on the Clyde – the ship-building and the iron-works – it had a light manufacturing tradition based on a wide range of craft industries. The figures may seem surprising to those who think of the city as a predominantly professional or administrative centre: from the mid nineteenth century to the middle of the twentieth century, about half the working male population of Edinburgh was involved in industry, with about one in three men in that group being engaged in manufacturing. In the same period, only one in six men earned their living in a professional capacity – as teachers, lawyers, bankers and so on. Of course these were the people from whom one heard, so to speak, with the result that their Edinburgh dominated the very different Edinburgh of those working in industry. And there may still be an element of that. Lawyers have a way of making their presence felt, and the social and political influence of the legal profession in Edinburgh has been immense – out of all proportion to the actual numbers of people engaged in the law. That has not necessarily been a bad thing: had the city been traditionally dominated by bankers and financiers it would have had a rather different atmosphere, certainly once banking and finance became infected with recklessness and ruthlessness. One of the greatest disasters to affect Scotland in recent years was, after all, the product of precisely those vices. In relatively few years the whole edifice of financial probity that Edinburgh and Scotland represented was seriously undermined in this city by the actions of a small number of bankers. The architecture that the great Scottish banks created in Edinburgh is still there and is the very embodiment in stone of the values that Scottish banking had at its core. But what happened to the Bank of Scotland? It still has its branches in Edinburgh, but its great banking halls in St Andrew's Square are not what they used to be. And the same is true of bank branches. My first bank in Edinburgh was the British Linen Bank on the corner of South Bridge and the High Street. That was later taken over by the Bank of Scotland, but the bank premises themselves remained the same. The bank had a wonderful wooden counter – a massive, solid construction that inspired confidence in anybody who contemplated it. Money which passed across that counter would be well looked after – there could be no doubt about that. And off in one corner was the manager's office where, courteously but sternly, the bank manager would interview you if you allowed your student account to become overdrawn. Those interviews were awkward in the first few minutes but became warmer, indeed even enjoyable, as the manager then went on to reminisce about his experiences in the War. I remember him telling me about the discomfort of the sleeping arrangements on active service, including one occasion on which he had to sleep

The Bank of Scotland, South Bridge and the Royal Mile, c1992
This was a bank building – indeed, when I was a student, it was my bank building – and it has all the solidity and impressiveness that a bank building could want. The entrance was through the door on the right and the small banking hall within had a most beautiful hardwood counter. As has been the fate of many old bank buildings, it was turned into a hotel and a bar.
RCAHMS SC668478

It is a particular pleasure

suddenly

in a bath. What bank manager would entertain his young clients with such stories today? Indeed, what bank would have a manager who would even speak to the students with accounts at his branch?

The former Bank of Scotland branch on that corner has now become a bar. A similar fate has befallen one of the great banking halls in George Street. I suppose it could have been worse – at least they did not become casinos …

The industries that grew up in Edinburgh were generally on a smaller scale than those spawned by the industrial revolution in other major cities. Glass making, small chemical industries, rubber industries – these all flourished in Edinburgh, often around the Water of Leith, that provided the water for these light industrial processes and carried the resulting effluent away (or moved it downstream). The rubber industry was particularly important: the North British Rubber Company, which became the Scottish Vulcanite Company, was set up in Fountainbridge in 1855 and in due course made Edinburgh a leading world producer of rubber products in the second half of the century. These industries were eventually encouraged to go to industrial zones within the city – there was one around Dalry and one around Easter Road. These attracted housing – and football clubs: the Heart of Midlothian grounds at Tynecastle and those of Hibernian at Easter Road. All Edinburgh, of course, knows the religious division that these clubs reflected, Hearts being Protestant and Hibs being Catholic. The tragedy of sectarianism never blighted Edinburgh in the way

in which it harmed some other parts of Scotland, but it was there nonetheless.

Crafts were extremely important in the city's industrial landscape, and continued to be so throughout the nineteenth century. These industries were integrated into the sinews of the city itself, rather than being relegated to specifically industrial areas, with the result that Edinburgh has always had small clusters of workshops existing cheek by jowl with flats and houses. It is a particular pleasure to walk along an ordinary street and suddenly discover a bagpipe maker's workshop. You used to be able to do that, and I think it is still possible, as bagpipe makers have not disappeared entirely. More prosaically, the premises of shoe repairers or plumbers will often be right next to the doorway of a common residential stair, thus perpetuating that mixture of work and everyday life that makes for a human city. When I walk into town along Brunstfield Place, for example, I pass, in rapid succession, a French bakery, a newsagent, a butcher, the entrance to flats, a tailoring workshop, more doorways into flats, a hairdresser, a coffee shop, another coffee shop: it is a far cry from the sterility of streets that are given over to one thing and one thing alone.

These small concerns may have been important, but there were some large industries too, notably printing and brewing. Printing is an industry I love for the sheer romance of the actual process – a press is a wonderful piece of equipment – and for its association with literature

to walk along an ordinary street and discover a bagpipe maker's workshop

and ideas. At the end of every writer's labours there is an actual industrial process involving machines that make a noise and ink that actually smells. Some writers may not be interested in all that, but ever since, as a boy of eight, I was given my first John Bull Printing Set I have been fascinated by printing. The John Bull Printing Set consisted of small wooden blocks into which rubber type might be set. That then created a stamp that enabled you to print a few lines: your address, usually, or some brief message in blurred ink. Later I acquired an Adana printing machine – a compact domestic press capable of printing small pages – and eventually a proper platen press that I bought for £30 from a printer in Thistle Street who was getting rid of his old equipment. That printer had several beautiful old presses in his works, including one surmounted by a large gilded metal eagle – a machine of quite exceptional beauty. Today, of course, we can all be printers with our desktop publishing programmes and our laser printers, but such things will never match the satisfaction of impressing metal type on paper.

Printing in Edinburgh started in 1507, with the earliest press being at the Cowgate end of Blackfriars Street; by 1910 there were 400 booksellers and stationers in the city and 40 printers' firms. For centuries bookselling, printing and publishing all went together: Allan Ramsay, the father of the artist, was an example of a bookseller who in the early eighteenth century published and printed the books he sold; he had premises in the High Street before he moved to the Luckenbooths. With industrialisation the size of printing firms increased and the old printer/publisher became a thing of the past. The course was now set for Edinburgh to became one of the most important printing centres in the world, printing for the entire British Empire. If the name of Glasgow firms could be found on boilers and engines in the most remote spots, then the name of Edinburgh printing firms would similarly be found on books throughout the English-speaking world.

The names of these Edinburgh firms are well-known to anybody interested in the history of printing and of the book: Oliver and Boyd, James Ballantyne and Co, T & A Constable, Thomas Nelson – these were all illustrious firms whose work spanned the nineteenth and twentieth centuries. Oliver and Boyd, one of the most distinguished of these, had famous premises in Tweeddale Court, off the High Street. From this attractive building, just a short passageway from the bustling High Street, they published writers such as James Hogg and Thomas Carlyle. In the late 1970s this building was rescued by my friend Robin Hodge, who rolled up his sleeves and brought back to life a piece of Edinburgh's architectural heritage that had been allowed to decline. Now it was ready for use again as a centre of publishing, and Canongate Press, which had previously occupied a tiny office round the corner in Jeffrey Street, moved in. That was joined by the magazine Robin publishes, *The List*, thus returning the building to its earlier use. I was associated with Canongate in its Jeffrey Street days. It was an office that

The redoubtable waiting staff of the Doric Tavern, 1973

This was the regular lunchtime stop for the *Scotsman* newspaper staff. Liquid lunches were sometimes supplemented with food. I remember the ladies shown in this photograph; they represented everything that was great about Scotland.

Scotsman Publications, Licensor Scran

was always full to the brim with manuscripts, proofs, and designs for book jackets. At its centre sat a publisher of rare genius – Stephanie Wolfe-Murray, who had a talent for spotting manuscripts that would make gravely beautiful books. But she also had an endearing talent for temporarily mislaying manuscripts; when concerned authors telephoned to find out the verdict on their submission, the secretary would say 'Your manuscript is under active consideration', which meant 'We are actively looking for your manuscript'.

Edinburgh is still a publishing centre, although its fortunes as such declined in the twentieth century. Not only did the city lose many of its printing works, but it also lost a number of firms that published on any real scale. This was a tragedy for the city that, after all, printed and published the first edition of the *Encyclopaedia Britannica*. And yet the strong attachment that the city has to the book and its production was not to be crushed, and small publishers have popped up like spring flowers. Today there are still publishers of note in the city, and one of them, Birlinn, the largest of the Scottish-based general publishing firms, has its headquarters in Newington, an area of the city that has always been associated with printing and publishing. Just round the corner was the famous map publisher, John Bartholomew, and Newington, we might remember, is also where Roget of *Roget's Thesaurus* once lived (flourished, inhabited, existed).

There is still scholarly and scientific publishing: until they moved to new offices in Holyrood, Edinburgh University Press published from atmospheric, but extraordinarily cramped offices in George Square. Atmosphere and space do not always co-exist: I had many meetings in an office in the building that I thought had once been a cupboard. And for so long so many Edinburgh offices were like that – even in the case of well-set legal and financial firms in Charlotte Square and elsewhere in the New Town. But that did not matter. Big offices can encourage big egos, which is not what one necessarily wants. There is something rather charming about a city that expects important people to work in cupboards.

And then there is the *Scotsman*, the newspaper that since its first publication in 1817 has been at the centre of the city's conversation with itself, with Scotland, and indeed with the rest of the world. It is hard to imagine Edinburgh without the *Scotsman*, just as it is hard to imagine North Bridge without the old Scotsman offices. These offices have become a hotel, the fate of many important buildings when their original purpose is overtaken by changes in society – churches become houses, banks become bars, schools and libraries become leisure centres, or gyms, or commercial stores. The Plaza Ballroom in Morningside became a supermarket; I suppose if people met in ballrooms they will also meet in supermarkets, although somehow such meetings will seem less romantic than those that took place on the dance floor. Edinburgh does not strike me as the sort of place for that quintessentially American invention, the singles' shopping night, but perhaps these occur, even if informally.

Down the side of the Scotsman building are the Scotsman steps. Like most, I used to avoid these unless I needed to get down to Market Street *celeriter* and without bothering about what one might encounter on the descent. I much preferred the route at the back of the building, a straight set of steps that ran past an ancient hairdressing establishment, a bar, and then the mighty printing rooms of the newspaper itself. You would hear the sound of the presses and smell the printer's ink – a delicious, evocative smell. Then down at the bottom would be the delivery vans ready to take the *Evening News* off to a hundred small newsagents' shops around the town. Turn left, and you were at the Doric Tavern which used to be presided over by Mr McGuffie, who with old-fashioned courtesy welcomed you to his dining room on the first floor – all gingham-covered tables and journalists enjoying the sort of lunch (largely liquid) that journalists today can only dream about. Mr McGuffie's waitresses tended to be fairly aged

– wonderful characters each of whom carried in their heads a lot of history of the town in general and of the people who lunched and dined in the Doric. And it was not just journalists who frequented the place, but others, such as that remarkable man of letters, Owen Dudley Edwards, a kind man and inspirational teacher at the University, who writes on Sherlock Holmes and American history and a hundred other topics. Owen is a Dubliner but adopted Edinburgh and became an integral part of the political and literary resurgence of the late seventies and eighties.

The *Scotsman* was badly affected by the change in reading habits that saw the circulation of so many newspapers tumble. Fat was cut off until it seemed that none remained, but at least the newspaper continues. So there is still somewhere for Edinburgh to conduct the debates that any society must have – to argue about the parish pump and the wider world, to allow for people to sound off and complain, to discuss things like the climbing of Munros and recipes for shortbread and the pros and cons of wind power. Without it, Scottish life would be greatly impoverished, and Edinburgh would lose, if not all its voice, then at least a major part of it.

The Southern Motors Filling Station, Causewayside, 1933
Designed by a young Sir Basil Spence, this is one of the few Art-Deco filling stations to be seen in Scotland. The building envisaged here in Spence's original perspective drawing survives today – although it now serves a rather different kind of refueling, as a thriving wine store. The car has always been an afterthought in Edinburgh, unlike those cities where it has dictated the shape of things.
Royal Incorporation of Architects in Scotland, RCAHMS DP004289

The Edinburgh Fruit, Vegetable and Fish Market, below North Bridge, 1829

This is a remarkably clean view of Edinburgh's sprawling central market – its stalls and traders filling the space occupied today by the great expanse of Waverley Railway Station. This engraving was produced for the book *Modern Athens*, and was part of the publicity drive to present Edinburgh as the successor to classical Greece. The reality of the nineteenth century city and its markets was a great deal more 'earthy' and visceral than this image suggests – a lot closer, one suspects, to the 'stinking ravine' filled with 'gin-drinking women' and packs of aggressive butchers' dogs that Henry Cockburn described.
Thomas H Shepherd, RCAHMS SC465097

A horse market in the Grassmarket, 1905

The names of businesses on buildings provide us with a commercial and industrial history of cities. It is striking how long buildings remain in the same hands or fulfil the same purpose. The Beehive Hotel, shown here as a backdrop to this horse market scene, is still there, although it is now a pub. There is a notice on the left which is difficult to decipher. It makes some reference to 'working men'. The Grassmarket always had working men's hostels sitting next to inns, and was a place of refuge and retreat for those down on their luck. The horses for sale here appear to be dray horses of some sort. That they were used to deliver milk is something still within living memory in Edinburgh. They probably also delivered beer, as the city's many breweries employed large teams of horses.
Robert Dykes, RCAHMS DP095099

340

BELL WIG MAKER & HAIR CUTTER

The Lawnmarket, 1873

At number 340, Bell Wig Maker and Hair Cutter offered his services in the shadow of the Castle, near the very top of the West Bow. This timber-fronted, gabled house was probably built in the sixteenth century, but was finally demolished and replaced in 1878. Above Bell's premises, each successive floor of the building seems to be larger than the one below it – a sign perhaps, of the Old Town hierarchy, where the richer residents lived at the top of houses, and in more spacious accommodation, than the poorer people below. Daniel Wilson, RCAHMS SC426625

James Souter's Shop,
Old Playhouse Close, 1936

Now here's a useful shop. James Souter offers 'Drysaltery' (chemicals including glue, varnish and dye), 'Hardware' and 'Fancy Goods'. The three tin baths hanging on the right are graded in size. The top bath was obviously for those whom prosperity had favoured. Above the shop next door is a typical sign which can still be seen throughout the city – remaining even after proprietors have left and their businesses have closed down: 'newsagent, tobacconist, confectioner'. One of the newspaper boards on the far right, below the front window, offers some interesting advice. RCAHMS SC1103837

Marcus Furs, Frederick Street, 1955

This shows the more elegant side of retail in Edinburgh. There were many fur shops in the city, when Edinburgh had a reputation for having more fur coats than anywhere else. Those disappeared very suddenly as fur became unpopular. Across the valley of Princes Street Gardens we see the snow-covered roofs of the Ramsay Garden flats. These buildings contain some of the most beautiful properties in Edinburgh, enjoying magnificent views to the north. The drawback of living there has always been what happens in August. Massed piped bands play outside their windows every evening during the famous Military Tattoo. And there is no point in going to bed before the fireworks are set off.

Tom and Sybil Gray, RCAHMS SC679801

China and Glass Gallery and advertisement for Jenner's Department Store, c1900

These images of Jenner's show the proud side of Edinburgh. The advertisement points out that Jenner's provided the carpets for what was then the North British Hotel on the other side of the road. It discreetly reminds us that these carpets are of 'exceptional merit'. Try reading that lower note in a 'Morningside' accent – it sounds perfect. Henry Bedford Lemere, RCAHMS SC678369 and RCAHMS DP151350

Jenner's defines a certain kind of Edinburgh, and I have attempted to capture this in a song, put to

In Jenner's Tea Room

Seated at table in Jenner's Tea Room,
The ladies of Edinburgh take afternoon tea,
Cups and saucers in fine English china,
Three good friends and one invitee.

Mrs Abernethy, who's clearly their leader,
Serves out the sandwiches, two to a plate,
Makes sure that the cake is cut quite thinly
(Mrs Abernethy keeps an eye on her weight.)

'And so, Mrs Donald,' she asks of her neighbour,
'Is it Elie again, as it is every year?'
The quiet Mrs Donald whispers her answer:
'It'll be terribly crowded, and breezy, I fear.'

Mrs Abernethy has several daughters,
And one of them has a young man in tow;
'He's not a Watsonian,' confesses the matron,
'In fact I believe that he comes from Glasgow!'

The other three ladies are quite sympathetic,
It could happen, they say, to any of us,
But in spite of it all there's still Jenner's Tea Room,
Where everything's done with so little fuss.

Once tea is over all of the ladies
Get out their diaries to fix the next date;
At Jenner's again? At three for three-thirty?
And with that, I'm afraid, there's no more to relate.

Montage of Princes Street facades, running east to west from St David's Street (top right) to Frederick

Princes Street before the architectural disaster hit. Many of these attractive buildings have been replaced with soulless structures of the sort

reflect the history or feel of the city. Fortunately the stately building of Jenner's, pictured here top right bedecked with flags, survives. In the

"THE "LIFE" ASSOCIATION OF SCOTLAND"

BUYER AND SELLER OF
ANTIQUES AND FINE JEWELS

JENNER'S

Waverley Railway Station,
1950 and 2013

Trains once steamed in and out of Waverley   Scotland, reappears briefly as it runs through the

Princes Street Railway Station, Lothian Road, 1966 and 1950

There is a melancholy feel about quiet or deserted railway stations. The solitary figures in these two highly atmospheric photographs are caught in the same way as the subjects in an Edward Hopper painting. Cities can be lonely places. The image on the right shows the station in 1950 while it was still in use. On the left,

however, it had already been closed down. No trains would arrive at these platforms again, and the station, which served the west end of Princes Street, was demolished not long after the photograph was taken.

The *Scotsman*, Licensor Scran

Tom and Sybil Gray, RCAHMS SC679143

The North British Hotel, c1930

This great stately hotel is so utterly confident. It
presides here over the comings and goings at the
east end of Princes Street. It was just this sort of
scene, with the street outside lined with what look
like expensive cars – 'muckle-big municipal Rolls-
Royces' – that inspired the poet Robert Garioch
to remark that the hotel 'gives our toon some
tone, you'll all agree'.
Francis Caird Inglis, Scottish Colorfoto,
RCAHMS SC466207

WAVERLEY   MARKET   FAÇADE

Competition design drawing for the North British Hotel, 1895

The hotel's location as the eastern anchor of Princes Street has made it one of Edinburgh's most recognisable landmarks. As is often the case with major buildings, however, there were many possibilities for what it could have looked like. This drawing of the western facade was part of a competition entry by the architects Dunn and Findlay. Note, in particular, the absence of the now famous clock tower. The zigzag line running diagonally down the facade represents the Waverley Steps – the characterful route, and notorious wind-tunnel, that links the station platforms to Princes Street.

Dunn and Findlay, RCAHMS DP007781

The Banks of Edinburgh

Banks should look like this. These buildings demonstrate solidity, caution, respect for tradition, and permanence. Scottish banking enjoyed a very high reputation for all of these qualities, even though that reputation was tarnished during the banking scandals of the early twenty-first century. The people who worked in these buildings would have been shocked to the core by what happened during the recent financial crisis.

top left
Perspective Drawing of Edinburgh Savings Bank, Hanover Street, 1938
Cyril Farey, RCAHMS SC712285

bottom left
Architect's drawing of the Royal Bank of Scotland, 42 St Andrew's Square, c1934
Leslie Grahame Thomson, MacDougall Collection, RCAHMS SC691952

top right
Engraving of the Royal Bank of Scotland, St Andrew's Square, c1830
Thomas H Shepherd, RCAHMS DP095278

bottom right
Engraving of the Bank of Scotland Headquarters on the Mound, 1805
R Scott, RCAHMS DP094898

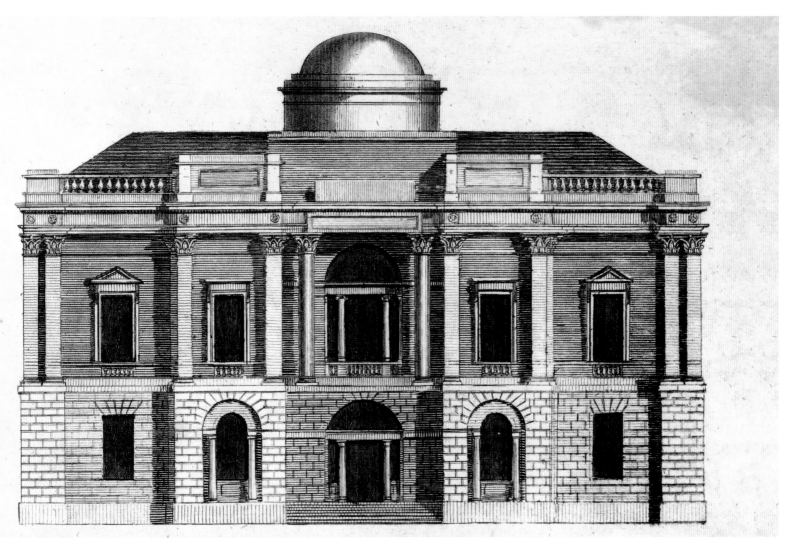

The Banking Hall of the British Linen Bank, St Andrew's Square, 1890

This magnificent photograph shows the full splendour of this great banking hall. Designed in 1846 by the architect David Bryce, the detail in the decoration is extraordinary and very fine materials have been used, including polished Peterhead granite for the substantial columns, engraved glass, and Minton floor tiles. There is an almost religious quality to this architecture – a sanctification of the business being conducted beneath the great glass dome. In here, it suggests, money is sacred.

Henry Bedford Lemere, RCAHMS SC700912

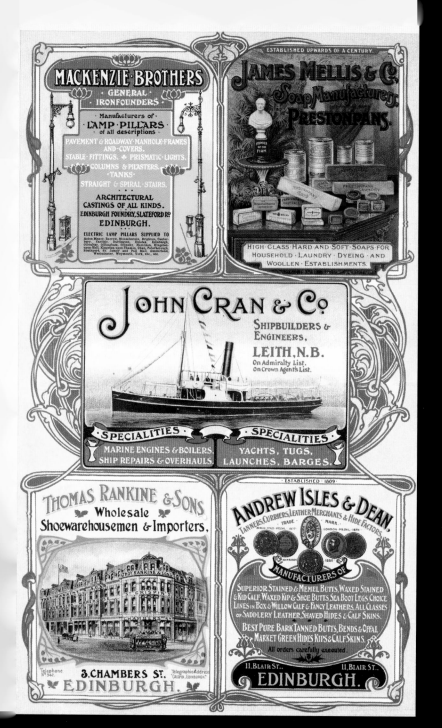

Scotland's Industrial Souvenir, 1905

Published in 1905, this trade catalogue promoted the diverse range of products manufactured in Scotland, with advertisements for goods ranging from soap, sacking and smoked fish, to boiler brushes, heavy engineering and horseshoes. Over 6,000 copies were sent to

and Boards of Trade in every part of the world. Copies were also included as reading material onboard Cunard ocean liners travelling to far flung locations like South Africa and Japan. The number of Edinburgh businesses taking advertisements in the catalogue is testament

unappreciated – role as a centre of manufacturing. In the images here, there are enticements to buy lampposts, shoes, glue, yachts, toilet brushes, and turnips: an eclectic mix. The advertisement for the George Street store of James Gray & Son will resonate with many Edinburgh people who used

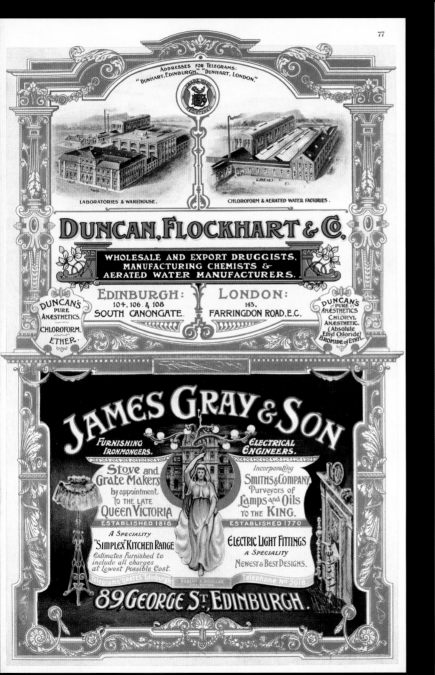

The New Street Gasworks, Canongate, 1868, 1910 and 1930

A city's landmarks can change dramatically over time. Some structures, which appear to speak so loudly of permanence, often make just fleeting intrusions into the urban fabric. Such was the fate of the gigantic chimney in the centre of these images. It was part of the gasworks on New Street, near the foot of the Royal Mile – which, for a time, supplied gas to almost the entire city. Depicted here first in an engraving from 1868 – with other chimneys in the background – the following images show the change in the skyline over time. By 1930, it is one of the few tall chimneys remaining. In the last image, the roof bears the slogan 'the "Help" factory, under the management of the distress committee'. This is neither graffiti, nor an SOS from the ailing gasworks, but rather a sign that the business in question was offering work to those who were unemployed and in financial difficulties.

left – RCAHMS DP033102

bottom left – Scottish Colorfoto, RCAHMS SC1167307

top right – Francis M Chrystal, RCAHMS SC1131441

right
Dean Village from the Dean Bridge, c1910

Before Edinburgh expanded, the Dean Village sat to the north of the city as its own, somewhat isolated, community. In many ways, this is how it remains today. Its location – nestled in the steep-sided river valley of the Water of Leith – has prevented any great changes or developments. While it is no longer, as it once was, a hugely productive milling village, its fabric and character has been remarkably well preserved.
H D Wylie, RCAHMS SC533143

'Scotsman' Buildings 'Block A'
North Elevation and Section H.
Drawing No 12

**Design drawing for
the Scotsman building, c1900**

What a splendidly iconic building from which
to issue an opinion-forming newspaper. This
building is clearly intended to be a working office,
but there are *jeux d'esprit* at the top – stone
adornments, domes and turrets. To the right
can be seen the close that still takes one up
from Market Street to Cockburn Street, an easy
descent but not so easy after a good lunch at
the nearby Doric Tavern. At the centre are the
'Scotsman Steps', which joined Market Street to
the North Bridge. Although a civically spirited
idea, these steps acquired a rather insalubrious
atmosphere – and were only to be navigated by
the brave after dark.
Dunn and Findlay, RCAHMS SC587781

**The Scotsman dispatch vans,
Market Street, 1956**

In our digital age we forget how physical a business
spreading the news used to be. The vans in this
ordered line are ready to take the *Scotsman* off
to its readers. They are parked right beside the
doorway behind which the great presses rolled.
When the paper was being printed there was
always the roar of the machinery to be heard in
this part of Market Street.
The *Scotsman*, Licensor Scran

Of Doctors

and Scientists

Edinburgh is a medical city.

Reputations can be very long lasting, and even if today the Nobel Prizes for Medicine are likely to go to those working in better-funded laboratories abroad, people throughout the world still associate the city with medical excellence. That reputation, of course, is well justified: Edinburgh has two of the United Kingdom's great medical colleges; it still mints specialists of all sorts; and it continues to be an important centre of medical research. The stock image of the Scottish doctor, found in the most remote and unexpected places – similar to the Glaswegian ship's engineer, found toiling in the engine-room of far flung ships – has, like so many such images, a basis in truth. Scotland has always exported doctors, and a good proportion of these have been Edinburgh-trained.

I have been reminded of this in odd circumstances. Some years ago I was admitted to a hospital in the middle of Kuala Lumpur after having swallowed a fish bone. As I was wheeled into the surgery (past, I could not help but observe, an illuminated sign that said, forebodingly, *Exit*), I was reassured by the masked Malaysian doctors by my side: 'Don't worry, we're all Edinburgh men'. Then, more recently, I paid a visit to a remote part of New Zealand's North Island, where my grandfather, a graduate of the Edinburgh Medical School, had spent most of his medical career, working in a Maori community. I had not visited his hospital before, but it was still there and there were

photographs and a portrait of him on the wall. He was ultimately responsible for the introduction of free medicine in that part of New Zealand, for which he fought with the utter determination of the resourceful Highlander that he was. I was touched by the traditional Maori welcome I received, and by the thought that his achievement there was the result of what he had been taught in Edinburgh. One elderly man stood up and said: 'he was a good doctor. If you were not too sick he could be brisk, but if you were really sick, my goodness, he never left your side. He would sit there with you all night if necessary.'

The Edinburgh medical story goes back a long way, but the reign of James IV is as good a starting point as any. James was the early sixteenth century Scottish king who came to an untimely end at the Battle of Flodden, that most poignant Scottish tragedy. He had a strong interest in science and medicine and liked to experiment, most famously, perhaps, by placing two infants on an island with a mute nurse. The aim of this bizarre venture was to see whether they would naturally start speaking Hebrew, in his view the natural language of humanity. Other experiments were a bit more grounded, and rather more likely to get ethics committee approval – had such things existed then. Some involved medical treatments, many of which probably hastened the patient's end, but a few may even have been of some benefit. Being treated by the king was not only a privilege, but could be profitable. His accounts recorded money given to a man who agreed that, with the king as his

Edinburgh Royal Infirmary, Lauriston Place, c1950
This photograph of a ward in the Royal Infirmary was taken around 1950. The National Health Service was then in its infancy. The light and the airiness of this room are quite striking – as is the presence of the grand piano.
H D Wylie, RCAHMS SC1124666

dentist, he should have 'twa teeth drawn furth of his heid'. James had his alchemists, too, and spent money and time in pursuit of the transformation of base metal into gold, just as we spend large sums today – on better grounds, of course – in pursuit of the arcane secrets of physics.

Even if the king's scientific experiments were not conspicuously successful, he made a lasting contribution to medicine by giving a royal charter to the Incorporation of Surgeons and Barbers of Edinburgh, a year after that body had been set up by the Town Council. Royal patronage in those days was very important in practical terms, and meant more than a nod of approval. Indeed, it helped to launch Edinburgh on the journey that was to make it at one point one of the leaders of medicine not only in the United Kingdom but also throughout the world. That enduring medical heritage is still evident in today's city, which is an important international centre for medical education and research. The old medical school may today be largely empty of students, and the Royal Infirmary over which it looked may now be luxury flats, but there are still medical buildings in use in much the same way that they were in the nineteenth century. This gives Edinburgh medicine a flavour of stability and wisdom: Edinburgh is not the place for the quick fix, the dubious theory, or the exploitation of the sick or the vulnerable – its medical traditions are very different from all that.

Two colleges formed the backbone of the Edinburgh medical world – the College of Surgeons and the College of Physicians. The surgeons were originally based in a tenement in Dickson's Close, later moving to the more salubrious surroundings of Curryhill House, in the south-west of the city. Here they conducted their public dissections, usually performed on the bodies of condemned criminals, events that provided a gruesome but popular spectacle. The status of surgeons was raised with their split from the barbers, and also by the increasing sophistication of their methods and the resources at their disposal. The new Surgeon's Hall, built on the site of its predecessor, eventually reflected the status of the profession in a Playfair-designed building of impressive columns and grand entrances. I have visited the college on many occasions ranging from medical Burns Suppers to medico-legal meetings, but have managed to avoid visiting its famous museum in which the tools of the surgical trade are displayed. This is not a failure to appreciate the work that the surgeons undertook, but stems more from an awareness that much of this work used to be done in a time before anaesthetic.

Which, of course, was an Edinburgh invention – or almost. Early steps in anaesthesia had been taken elsewhere, but it was in Edinburgh, at the house of James Young Simpson at 52 Queen Street, that Dr Simpson, together with his friends Dr Keith and Dr Duncan, experimented with chloroform and discovered its ability to put people to sleep. The image of three Edinburgh doctors sniffing drugs in a New Town dining room is

The Library of the Royal College of Physicians, c1865

The architect David Bryce was appointed to extend the College in the second half of the nineteenth century. This perspective proposal for the new library – which was completed in 1877 – will be familiar to many Edinburgh couples: for decades it has played host to countless wedding ceremonies and receptions. Royal Incorporation of Architects in Scotland, RCAHMS SC808496

He suggested putting a sign on his front door saying 'Last Psychiatrist

an amusing one, but it was of course a moment of great importance in the history of medicine. The story that the first child delivered with chloroform was called Anaesthesia is, disappointingly, untrue.

The Royal College of Physicians of Edinburgh is a building in the same grand tradition as Surgeons' Hall. The incorporation of the physicians was not welcomed by the surgeons, who tried to prevent it. These blocking moves failed, though, and the College of Physicians based itself first in Physicians' Hall, in George Street, and then in the even more substantial building it now occupies in Queen Street. The library and main hall of that building has particular resonances for my wife and me – as it does for many other Edinburgh couples – as it was here that we held the reception that followed our wedding.

At the heart of Edinburgh medicine has been the training of doctors. Until the medical school was founded in Edinburgh in 1726, medical education in the city was a very patchy affair, even if there were a few professors at the University who had been appointed to teach subjects such as human anatomy. In practice, those wishing to study medicine did so abroad, in places such as Leiden, where there was a tradition of hospitality to students from Scotland. With the appointment of medical professors in Edinburgh, that trip no longer became necessary, and doctors could receive a full training without going abroad.

The professors who taught medicine in Edinburgh were a mixed bag. The system of appointment was hardly an open one, and many of them appear to have inherited their chairs. It was not uncommon for posts to be held by three or four generations of the same family: the Bell family, for instance, were presidents of the College of Surgeons from Benjamin Bell (great-grandfather) to Joseph (great-grandson). Similarly, four generations of the Monro family held the chair of anatomy over a period of 126 years. Anatomy, of course, had its scandals, largely brought about by the shortage of bodies for dissection. Two of Edinburgh's most infamous citizens – Burke and Hare – sought to remedy this deficiency by preying on vulnerable people in places like the Cowgate, overpowering them, and selling the bodies to anatomists such as Dr Robert Knox. The macabre story of Burke and Hare continues to haunt the city – a walk by night through the West Port or the Cowgate can very easily invoke the atmosphere in which their crimes were perpetrated.

Nepotism may have been rife, but so was talent. The second half of the eighteenth century saw Edinburgh physicians producing textbooks of medicine that were used internationally. The techniques and insights of the Enlightenment inspired many Scottish doctors of the period; William Smellie, whose *Treatise on the Theory and Practice of Midwifery* was the definitive work on the subject at the time, used careful measurement and recording to make obstetrics a science, while the contribution of John Hunter, William Cullen and Matthew Baillie all helped to establish the pre-eminence of Scottish medicine.

Before the Dean Bridge'

The growth in the population of Edinburgh in the nineteenth century led to public health challenges. Edinburgh was not a healthy place, with respiratory diseases and rickets resulting from the insanitary and unhealthy conditions in which people lived. The roots of ill health in adverse social conditions were well understood by Edinburgh medicine by the mid nineteenth century, and public health measures began to tackle the problem. In the twentieth century, social conditions were immensely improved, but there were still plenty of dark and dank slums in Edinburgh well after the Second World War. Edinburgh public health specialists did not give up: tuberculosis, in particular, was in their sights and with the efforts of people like Sir John Crofton, the disease that had been responsible for such a high proportion of deaths was brought under control. Those who remember Edinburgh cinemas in the 1960s will recall the strange ritual of the spraying of the cinema with disinfectant during the show. From the perspective of those occupying today's comfortable armchairs in the Dominion Cinema in Morningside, such things must seem to be part of a very distant world. But there will be many such moments in a city like Edinburgh, where the visible heritage of the past is so evident in the buildings that are still in everyday use.

The Royal Infirmary has now vacated its site on the edge of the Meadows and the great Stalinist building of the Simpson Memorial Pavilion has been demolished. Other hospitals have found other uses. Craig House, a splendid Scots baronial building on the brow of a hill in Colinton, used to be part of the Royal Edinburgh Hospital (the psychiatric hospital in Morningside). Craig House was an imposing place with a large wood-panelled hall complete with stags' heads. This, I was once told, was to make nineteenth century patients from the more prosperous classes feel at home when admitted for their melancholia, as depression was then called. I remember going to the annual psychiatrists' dance there (my wife had worked in psychiatry at the Royal Edinburgh). The junior psychiatrists put on an amusing show, singing *Old Macdonald had a Funny Farm*, which was much appreciated by the chief psychiatrist of the time. He lived in the remarkable house that clings to the cliffs at the south end of the Dean Bridge in the New Town. This bridge, with its towering vaulted arches, stands high above the Water of Leith, and unfortunately was popular for suicides. He had suggested that he might put a sign on his front door saying *Last Psychiatrist Before the Dean Bridge*. Doctors need their humour to allow them to do what is at times a very trying job. That was certainly understood by the well-known Edinburgh geriatrician Colin Currie, who in the 1970s and 1980s wrote a number of pseudonymous medical novels, including the comic *The Houseman's Tale*. Dr Currie was, of course, following in well-trodden footsteps: Scottish medical novelists have included the creator of Sherlock Homes, Arthur Conan Doyle, who was born in Edinburgh, and

Portrait of the 'father of geology', James Hutton, c1776

This painting of James Hutton is by Sir Henry Raeburn. Although it is a very striking picture it seems to me to be a little bit more static than many portraits by Raeburn, who painted quickly and managed to convey a real sense of life in his pictures.

Scottish National Portrait Gallery, Licensor Scran

A J Cronin, author of the novels on which the Dr Finlay's Casebook television series was based.

Not far from Craiglea is Craiglockhart House, now part of Edinburgh Napier University. Craiglockhart is perhaps one of the most famous of medical buildings in Edinburgh, as during the First World War it had been the Craiglockhart War Hospital for Officers. Two of its most distinguished patients were the poets Siegfried Sassoon and Wilfred Owen, who were both treated for what was then called shell shock by that remarkable and human psychiatrist and anthropologist William Rivers. This is the setting for Pat Barker's moving novel *Regeneration*, which recreates the world of the shattered men who were the hospital's patients. Another patient there was Robert Graves, whose beautiful memoir *Goodbye to All That* was the first thing I read, in my teens, about the First World War.

Although it is undoubtedly medicine that dominates Edinburgh's contribution to science, there are other fields in which the city has excelled. Two figures stand out: James Hutton in the eighteenth century and Peter Higgs in our own times. Hutton was born in Edinburgh and studied medicine there, as well as in Paris and Leiden. He came from a reasonably prosperous agricultural background, and for a time he farmed in East Lothian. His scientific interests, however, began to claim more of his time, and he left the management of his farms to others while he pursued his interest in the land on which he stood. This interest, first sparked by ditches and wells and by the fossils and rock formations he observed, prompted him to think about how the earth was formed. In 1770 he established himself in a house on St John's Hill in the Pleasance, from which he was able to look out over Salisbury Crags and Arthur's Seat. The Crags, where volcanic rock reaches up in straining outbursts, fascinated Hutton and inspired him to expound his theory of how the earth had evolved over time. These ideas, expounded by Hutton at meetings of the Royal Society of Edinburgh, were radical. The view prevailing at that point in the eighteenth century was that the earth had been created at a specific moment; Hutton saw no evidence for this, indeed everything he observed seemed to point to a contrary conclusion. He believed that the earth had developed its current form over a long period of change and decay, and that there was neither a beginning nor an end to it. His insight into how sedimentary and igneous rocks developed separately was obtained by examining more closely what he saw from the window of his Edinburgh house. This was the beginning of the modern science of geology, and the circumstances of its invention are something that we might still contemplate as we go for a walk in Holyrood Park and look up at the Crags and the great volcanic rump that is Arthur's Seat. Rather like Copernicus and Freud, Hutton changed our whole understanding of the world.

As did another resident of the Edinburgh New Town, the Nobel laureate Peter Higgs, whose famous Higgs boson was eventually discovered through the massive efforts of

Professor Peter Higgs, 2008
Photographers and painters like to portray Professor Higgs in close proximity to mathematical symbols. This is understandable. The genial and modest nature of this great physicist is well captured in this photograph.
Claudia Marcelloni CERN-GE-0804049-01

the great particle accelerator of CERN in Switzerland. An understanding of the Higgs boson is beyond most of us, and certainly it passes my comprehension entirely, but apparently it changes everything. I have taken the liberty of making mention of Higgs in my novels, which adds, I hope, to any reality they may claim, as this modest and unassuming man can be seen walking the same streets that my fictional characters walk. He has told me that he does

not mind this at all. Even if there may not be 50 men of genius strolling around the Mercat Cross any more, at least there is one great physicist walking along Heriot Row or Dundas Street. Both Hutton and Higgs can be seen in the Scottish National Portrait Gallery – Hutton immortalised by no less a painter than Henry Raeburn, whose studio was in the same street as the Gallery now is, and Higgs by the Edinburgh artist Lucinda McKay.

Surgeons' Hall, Nicolson Street, 1961
The imposing Greek-revivalist portico of Surgeon's Hall does not seem to have quite enough room. That is an interesting feature of some of Edinburgh's grand buildings – the compact nature of the city excludes great forecourts and the like. Through the entrances to the left and right each year go numerous doctors from all over the world, presenting themselves for the fellowship examinations. The Royal College of Surgeons in Edinburgh still plays a major role in spreading the medical influence of the city around the world.
Scottish National Buildings Record, RCAHMS SC1159975

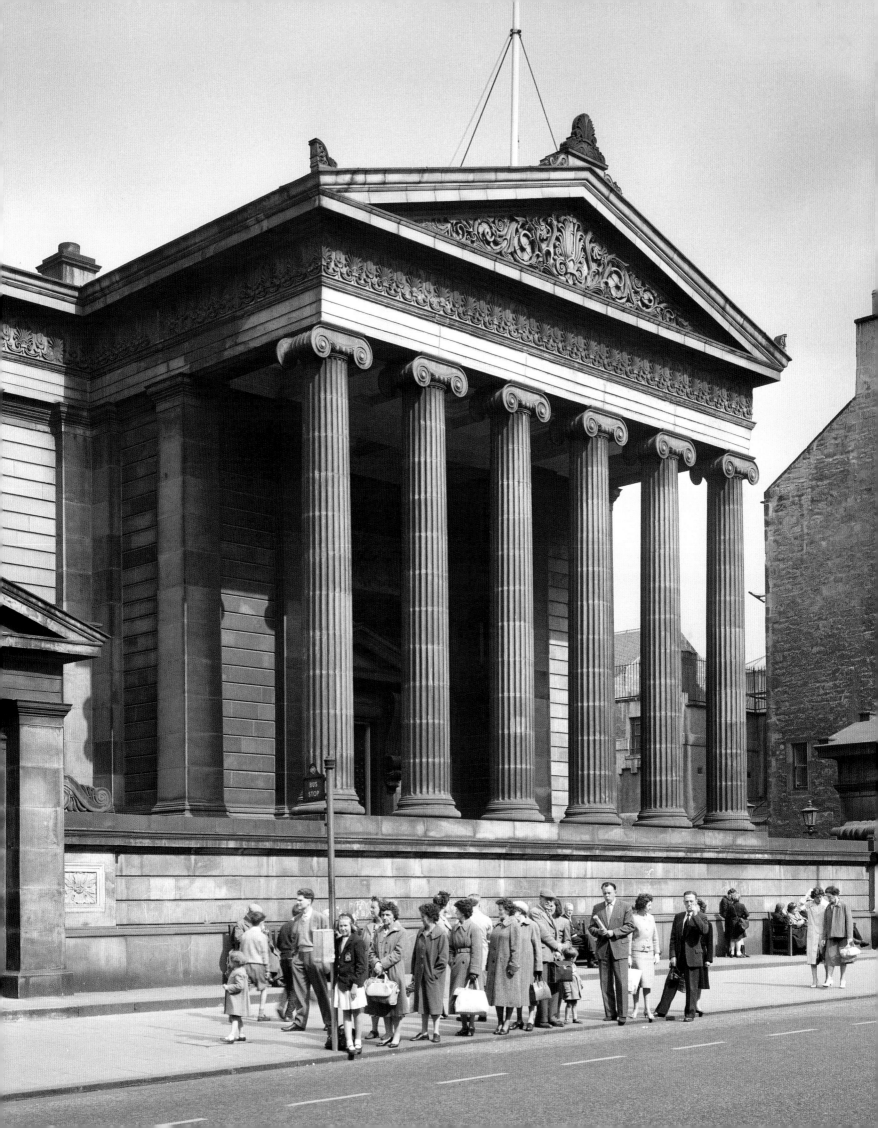

**The Exhibition Hall of the Medical
School of the University of Edinburgh,
Teviot Place, 1895**

Combining Victorian architecture with
skeletons is a sure recipe for a gothic scene, as
this atmospheric photograph demonstrates.
The collection on display in the Exhibition
Hall had anatomical specimens of every
conceivable nature, including elephants, wild
boars, apes, whales and dolphins. Today,
all but a handful of the remains have been
removed from this room, and it is now a
study space for students.
Henry Bedford Lemere, RCAHMS SC694690

Surgeons' Hall Museum, 1982

Set within William Playfair's elegantly designed galleries are some of the most gruesome and macabre objects in the history of Edinburgh. Not for the squeamish, they tell the important story of the development of anatomical knowledge and surgical techniques over the centuries – and of the city's often pioneering role in medical advances. Operating – sometimes quite literally – at the cutting edge can, however, invite scandal. The face we see in the display case on the left is the death mask of the notorious William Burke, who was executed for the provision of corpses for anatomical dissection – not insignificantly the corpses only became corpses through the efforts of Burke and his partner William Hare. As well as preserving Burke's face in plaster, the museum also exhibits his pocket book – or rather, a pocket book made out of his own skin, tanned into leather after his body was dissected by Alexander Monro, the University of Edinburgh's Professor of Anatomy.
RCAHMS SC942209

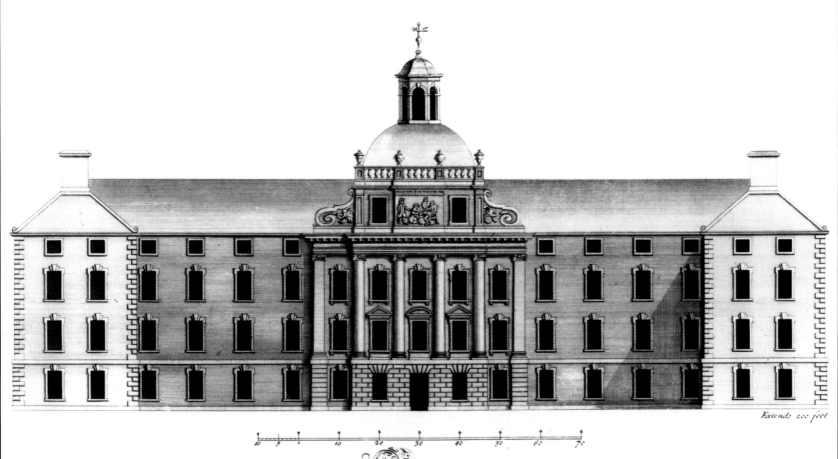

The North Front of the Royal Infirmary facing the City of Edinburgh

Gul: Adam inv: et delin

B. Cooper Sculp.

Extends 200 feet

**Old Royal Infirmary,
Infirmary Street, c1738**

This drawing – plate number 150 from

Edinburgh's role as a centre of medical

Old Royal Infirmary, c1870 and 1884

By the 1870s, work was underway on the new hospital and the move away from the old building had begun. This first image from 1870 shows the rather deserted-looking hospital in situ – set back from the road of Infirmary Street. In the second image, the demolition is well advanced. Adam's facade is surrounded by rubble but is still standing.
Alexander Inglis, Scottish Colorfoto,
RCAHMS SC1023665
Thomas Ross, RCAHMS SC1173466

The Royal Infirmary, Lauriston Place, 1879, c1880 and 2014

The time of David Bryce's hospital has also now come and gone. This sprawling complex, featuring a series of towers and turrets, was set overlooking one of Edinburgh's main green spaces – known as the Meadows. Today there are rather more sunbathers (if they are lucky) than sheep, and the infirmary buildings have been converted into luxury flats, with new, modern glass towers rising alongside the old ward buildings.

left – G M Simpson, RCAHMS DP073937

bottom left – Illustrated London News, RCAHMS SC601345

right – RCAHMS SC194405

Female Ward Fifteen, top floor of Edinburgh Royal Infirmary, c1917

David Bryce, the architect of the Royal Infirmary, consulted with Florence Nightingale in his designs for the form and layout of his hospital wards. This photograph reminds us of the days when nurses and doctors wore uniforms. The medical white coat is now considered a health hazard and no modern nurse would tolerate the long skirts and head gear.

Dr G L Malcolm-Smith, RCAHMS SC647741

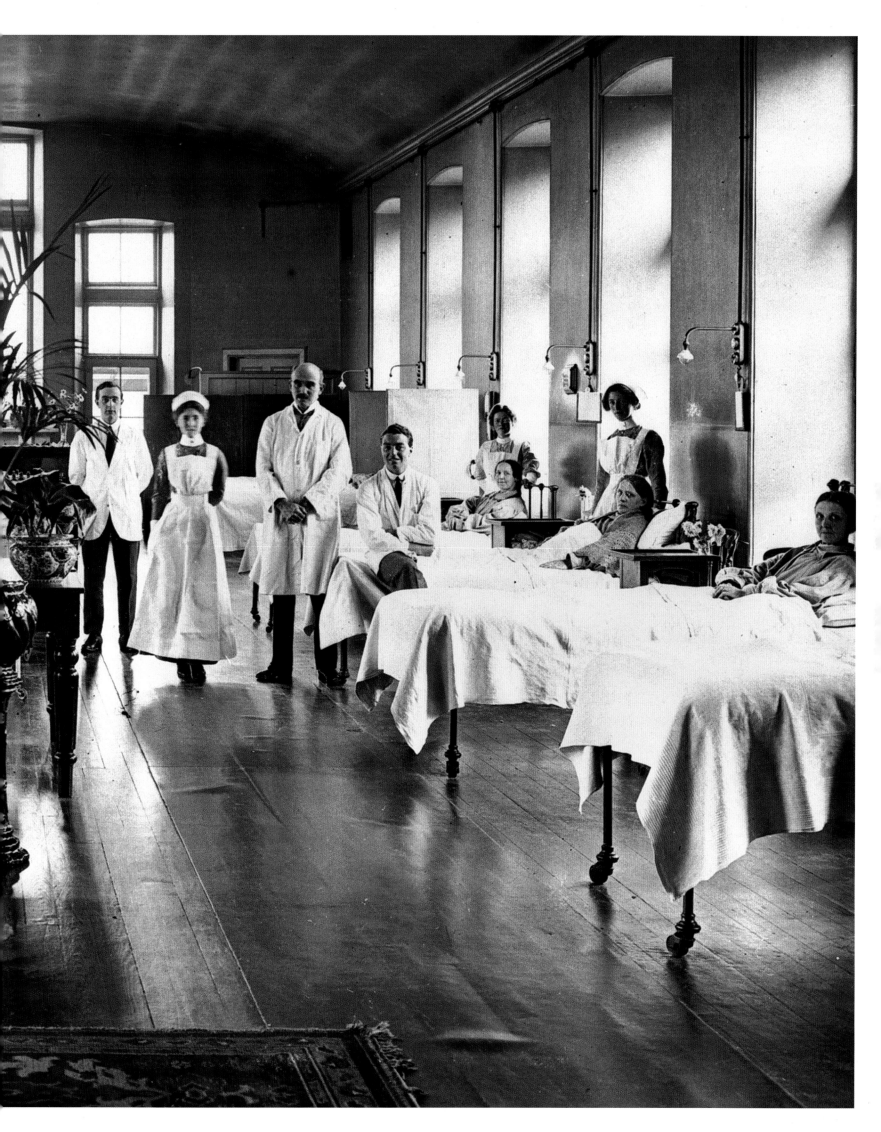

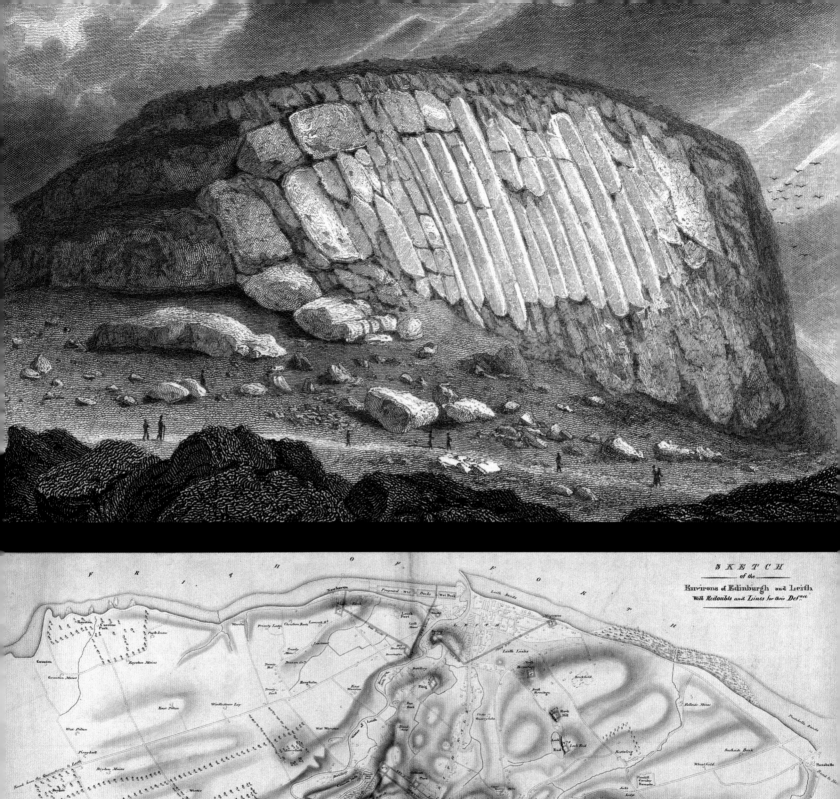

SKETCH
of the
Environs of Edinburgh and Leith
with Redoubts and Lines for their Defence

top left

Samson's Ribs, Arthur's Seat, c1830

From a geological point of view, Edinburgh wears its heart upon its sleeve. The exposure of rock formations associated with the volcano around which Edinburgh is built – now known as Arthur's Seat – helped James Hutton and others to understand the processes by which the earth's crust was formed. In a sense, the chance to discover a new science was waiting there, all around Hutton all the time. This engraving shows 'Samson's Ribs' – a row of six-sided columns of basalt rock that were formed many hundreds of thousands of years ago beneath the earth's crust.
Thomas H Shepherd, RCAHMS SC465108

bottom left

Sketch of Edinburgh and Leith, c1800

This drawing of the city and its surroundings, probably produced in the eighteenth century, is a military map showing forts, fortifications and lines of defence. It also works well as a topographical guide. Here we can see the massed cluster of peaks and troughs that dominate the city. Note in particular the great humps of Arthur's Seat, leading to the beak-like protuberance of Salisbury Crags; and the long thin and steep-sided line of the Old Town, stretching up to the Castle Rock. It is a reminder that one is never far from a slope or a summit in this city.
RCAHMS SC588896

top right

Edinburgh from Arthur's Seat, 1831

Few places can be viewed from such an unusual, and sometimes spectacular, vantage point as Edinburgh. As this engraving – one of a series of 'select views of cities of Europe' produced by Lieutenant-Colonel Batty – shows, Arthur's Seat provides a sweeping panorama of the urban landscape below. From here, one can watch the sun rise or set, and spot the rain rushing in across the Firth of Forth.
Edinburgh City Libraries, Licensor Scran

bottom right

Castle Rock from Princes Street Gardens, c1830

W Westall, RCAHMS DP094886

Edinburgh Castle

These are all different views of the Castle from various vantage points across the city. Unlike many capital cities, Edinburgh is not orientated around a great river. What it does have instead, however, is a wonderful central point to bring it together. The geology that made the Castle Rock an ideal place for a fortification also acts as a handy guide to those who might lose their bearings in Edinburgh's streets. Sooner or later, a glimpse of the Castle will help to guide wanderers in the right direction.

top left
Edinburgh Castle from Greyfriar's Kirkyard, c1930
Scottish Colorfoto, RCAHMS SC1240848

middle
The Vennel, with the Castle emerging from the mist, c1930
B C Clayton, RCAHMS SC1125101

bottom left
Ramsay Lane, looking up to the Castle, 1957
Tom and Sybil Gray, RCAHMS SC680475

right
Edinburgh Castle, looking over the Old Town to Arthur's Seat, 1951
Views of Edinburgh from the air can be like X-Ray photographs, showing the bones of the city. They reveal the spine that runs from the Castle to Holyrood, and reveal two limbs in the shape of Salisbury Crags and Arthur's Seat. Hutton looked at all of this from the ground, but if he were to see this aerial photograph, his vision would have been confirmed.
Aerofilms, RCAHMS SC1315250

next pages
A snow-clad Edinburgh Castle, viewed from Princes Street on a winter's day
Historic Scotland

Engraving of the Edinburgh Museum of Science and Art, now the National Museum of Scotland, c1890

This grand, Italianate building on Chambers Street began its life in the 1860s as the 'Industrial Museum of Scotland', but was soon renamed the 'Edinburgh Museum of Science and Art'. At the start of the twentieth century, it became the 'Royal Scottish Museum' and then, in the early years of the millennium, was rechristened the 'National Museum of Scotland'. One of the great delights of the interior is its soaring central atrium, pictured here in this engraving from 1890. A frame of structural cast-iron, based on the original Crystal Palace in Hyde Park, it has remained a fixture of the Museum even as the name has changed over the years. Many different objects and exhibits have been displayed beneath its glass roof, from Egyptian mummies to dinosaur skulls. Edinburgh people of a certain age will remember with great fondness the fishponds that once graced the centre of this magnificent public space, as well as the button-operated machines tucked away in the side galleries.
James Grant, RCAHMS SC834099

A view through the glass of an orrery on the second floor of the National Museum of Scotland, 2006
RCAHMS DP018171

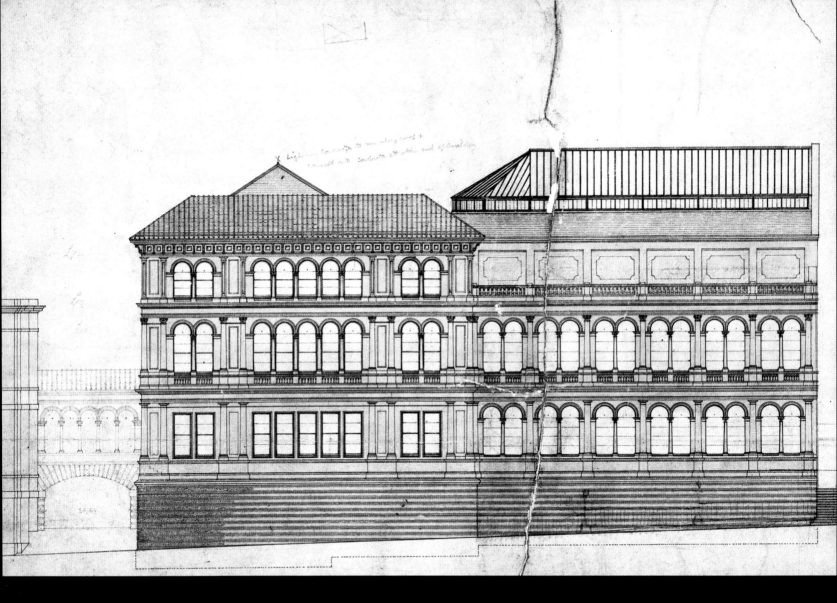

**Original design drawing for
the 'Industrial Museum
of Scotland', 1861**
Property Services Agency, RCAHMS SCI304450

**The National Museum
of Scotland, 2014**
In 2011, the old Victorian section of the Museum
re-emerged into Edinburgh life after a multi-
million pound refurbishment. Storage spaces
were turned into public spaces, and a great many

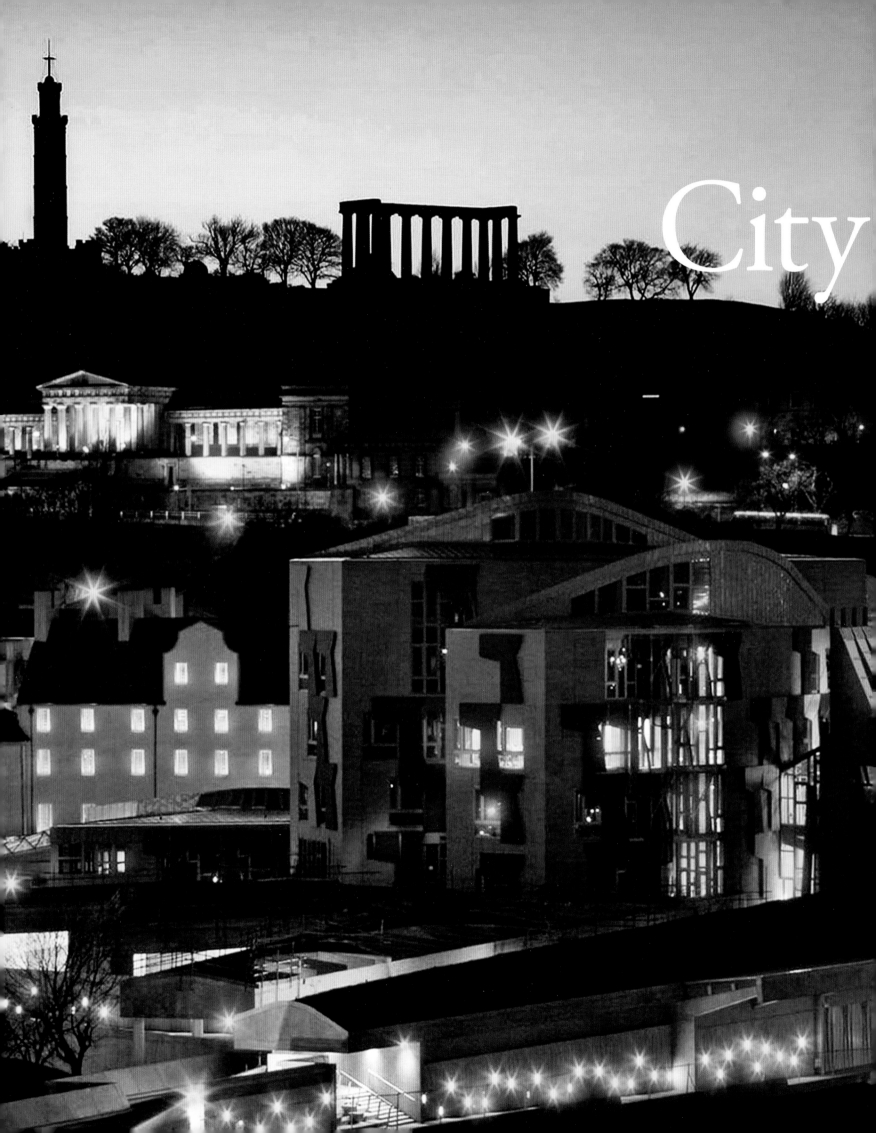

City

of the Mind

The life of the mind is every-where evident in Edinburgh.

This is a city given over to thinking and talking: wherever you go there are groups of people engaged in conversation – in the ubiquitous coffee bars, in pubs old and new, at Festival time in the rash of temporary artistic meeting places that pop up in the most unlikely places, in the new Scottish Parliament at Holyrood, pacing the floor of the old Parliament House, in corners and closes. And at night it is the same thing: in busy restaurants and at private dinners the talk continues, idle banter mixed with political argument and strong views, recollections, refutations, assertions, arguments good and bad, promises, lies, apologies, conspiracies – everything that goes to make up the life of an intellectually lively city.

Edinburgh's reputation as a city of the mind is founded on a remarkable single period in its eighteenth century history when it enjoyed the intellectual leadership of Europe. This was the period of the Scottish Enlightenment, that flowering of philosophy and related disciplines that for a while eclipsed what was happening elsewhere, even in much larger intellectual and academic capitals. During the Scottish Enlightenment, Edinburgh held its own with Paris, London, and the great German academic cities. With the Act of Union in 1707 Edinburgh may have lost its parliament, but the city did not lose its conceit of

itself and nor did it sink into provincialism. Indeed, in one view of 1707 – not necessarily the view held by all nationally minded Scots – the Union enabled Scotland to concentrate on the things that it could do well, which included intellectual endeavour. Of course that proposition is rejected by those who see 1707 as an ending rather than a beginning, but it is incontrovertibly true that Edinburgh experienced in the eighteenth century a remarkable Golden Age, and this has left its mark on the face of the city. The influence of the Enlightenment and Enlightenment figures is still very visible in Edinburgh – not only in statues and portraits, but in the very fabric of the town: in its shape, its look, its feel.

And the same may be said of its churches. Like the rest of Scotland, the hand of Christianity has been very active in the physical moulding of Edinburgh. The Church of Scotland may play a far smaller role in the life of the nation than it used to do in our more religiously observant past. Yet it is still there as a moral force in national life, and it reminds us of the spiritual dimension when the trumpets of materialism may seem to be drowning out other, gentler values. In the spring, the General Assembly of the Church takes place in the hall of New College, an imposing building on the Mound that sits cheek by jowl with the extraordinary red ashlar-dressed houses of Ramsay Garden. The General Assembly is still an important part of the national conversation on things that count – one of those rare opportunities for the nation to do its moral

Calton Hill, the Royal High School and the Scottish Parliament, 2005
Here, in three tiers descending from Calton Hill, are knowledge, learning, debate and discourse captured in architecture. Enlightenment monuments overlook the Royal High School built in the classical tradition and the twenty-first century Scottish Parliament – Scottish Parliament, Licensor Scran

philosophy in public. There is much ceremony, too, that reminds us that this is a variety of state occasion: the Lord High Commissioner, appointed by the Queen to represent her, is put up for the week of the Assembly in Holyroodhouse and gives receptions and dinners every night for Scotland's movers and shakers (or at least for the movers; shakers can be problematic) while visiting schools, hospitals and factories during the day. Through various hereditary ceremonial offices, representatives of the old Scottish nobility are in attendance, carrying standards and processing with due solemnity; there is a part of Edinburgh that still likes that sort of thing (and, in an increasingly homogenised world, colour of this sort surely relieves the monotony – and the monotone.) These are well-behaved descendants of a troublesome sector of Scottish society: the old Scottish nobles, of course, were not a particularly edifying group. With few exceptions, Scottish nobles of earlier times were in reality noted for their ruthlessness and bitter infighting, their eminence coming from their egregious ability to plunder rather better than anybody else. It was in this way that many grandees acquired their vast estates in Scotland: by taking land out of communal or church ownership and, in some instances, by forcing small farmers off the land and into the emigrant ships. Scottish history is painful – drenched in as large a volume of tears as of blood. And yet it *is* our history, and in these colourful Edinburgh ceremonies we see an important feature of Edinburgh's civic existence: the past is still at work – rather

than being distant and alien – we inhabit it in Edinburgh. It is in our streets and our buildings; it is in our rituals (such as they are); it is in the way we speak – the little expressions we use; it is in the names of streets and closes; it is in the faces that we can find if we look in the pages of Kay's *Edinburgh Portraits*. It is the same people who are about us, still there.

From the eminence of the High Kirk of St Giles', firmly astride the spine of the Old Town, to the modest churches tucked away on side streets, we are continually reminded that the Church was for many centuries at the very heart of the lives of Edinburgh's citizens. Sometimes this role was a baneful one: religious intolerance thrived in Scotland, as did ill-humoured squabbling and Protestant sectarianism. People were hounded for theological non-conformity or for failing to meet the Church's standards in their private lives; atheism was not countenanced. We might remind ourselves of the fact that it was in Edinburgh that Britain's last execution for heresy took place. This was the hanging in 1697 of the young student Thomas Aikenhead, who had been accused and convicted of publicly maintaining, among other heretical views, that theology was nonsense. 1697 – that is not all that many generations ago.

The Christian Church, of course, has changed out of all recognition from the church of John Knox and the zealots of the Reformation; the narrowness and rigidity of outlook has been replaced by something quite different, by charity and concern, by a gentleness of spirit and a healing social

The procession of the General Assembly of the Church of Scotland, Assembly Hall, 1954

The statue on the mid left of this photograph is John Knox. He is looking down here sternly – after all he is Calvinist – on a procession of the Lord Lyon and his colleagues dressed in all their finery. The General Assembly remains one of the most important occasions for Scottish pageantry.

The *Scotsman*, Licensor Scran

vision that is much more in accordance with the original spirit of a religion founded on *agape* – on 'unconditional love'. Many of the churches of Edinburgh, though, were erected in the period when Scottish Christianity was perhaps somewhat sterner, and this is reflected in the rather daunting, disapproving look of some churches.

And yet, and yet … as dreary as much church architecture may seem to some modern eyes, in spite of the blackened stone towers and the bone-chillingly poorly heated interiors, there may be a beauty to it that is truly spiritual. Edinburgh is fortunate in having several churches that seem imbued with a calm grace that has something to do with the egalitarian no-nonsense approach of Scottish Protestantism. That tradition is distrustful of ornament: icons and incense have been unpopular in much of Scotland, as has a theology that inserts a priest between the human and the divine. So Edinburgh's churches often embody a meeting hall style of architecture – an architecture that gives us the clean charm and airiness of somewhere like Canongate Kirk. Entering that church does not promote any sense of subservience or dread: rather it encourages an elation of the spirit. Here the proud would find it hard to be proud; here the unkind would find unkindness difficult; here the unity of community is celebrated – a spiritual citizenship is fostered. And that feeling, I think, would strike anybody going into the building, irrespective of religious faith.

From the churchyard at Canongate Kirk one looks out over an urban glen to Calton Hill, and its monuments. This is an eccentric skyline, a collection of attempts to commemorate and dignify – a great jumble of ideas and ambitions, realised and unrealised. The crowning glory is of course the National Monument, an unfinished attempt at recreating the Parthenon. That would have been part of Playfair's great scheme for the area – a scheme that would have rivalled the New Town for its grandeur and ambition, but it was not to be. And so now we have the beginnings, but only the beginnings, of something impossibly grand – a reminder, perhaps, of what Burns famously said about the best-laid plans of mice and men. Still, it looks rather good there, rather like one of those curious out-of-context installations in which modern conceptual artists take such delight. At night and at certain key times of the year, this is a good place for pagan festivals, at which people paint their faces blue and leap about, while just down the hill, in their New Town bedrooms, the respectable burgers of the town sleep the sleep of . . . the respectable burgers of the town. 'For those who like that sort of thing,' opined Miss Jean Brodie, 'well, that's the sort of thing they like.'

The National Monument had been intended to celebrate British victory in the Napoleonic Wars. There had been a similar ambition in England, where there had been plans to erect a Parthenon either in Trafalgar Square or Hyde Park. These were not fulfilled, and the idea was taken up in Edinburgh, where a group of supporters described as

Here the proud would find it hard to be proud

Canongate Kirk, 1799
The gabled front of Canongate Kirk makes a theological and aesthetic statement. Originally constructed in the late seventeenth century, there is a pleasing simplicity to this lovely building – John Elphinstone, RCAHMS DP189944

a 'numerous and respectable meeting of noblemen and gentlemen of Scotland' passed a resolution to erect 'a Temple of Gratitude to God, for the protection he had, in the day of peril, afforded to the Land, and for the Glory he has, in the day of Battle and of Victory, shed around the Warriors of Caledonia'. This appealed to the vanity of those Scots who saw Edinburgh as the intellectual heir of Ancient Greece – the Athens of the North, to use a soubriquet that was widely applied to the city. The Earl of Elgin – whose name is forever connected to the Parthenon through the eponymous Marbles – was a supporter of the idea, and it was at his suggestion that the English architect Charles Cockerell was involved in the project. Cockerell was a follower of Greek Revival ideas and was joined in the designing of the Parthenon by the Scot William Playfair, another Greek revivalist. They were both most enthusiastic, but not enough money could be raised and work stopped. This is what Playfair wrote to Cockerell:

> My Dear Cockerell … Our Parthenon is come to a dead halt. And is I am afraid likely to stand up a striking proof of the pride and poverty of us Scots. The masonry is as good as can be and the columns … when the sun shines and there is a pure blue sky behind them (a rare event you will say) they look most beautiful … What is to be done next I know not – I suppose *Nothing*.

Almost two hundred years later, Edinburgh engaged in another great project – the creation of a tram network, but ran out of money and ended up with something with more than a passing resemblance to an incomplete Parthenon. The same things happen in history – time and time again.

The cemetery by Calton Hill has an important little tower which has carved over the door the name: DAVID HUME. This is his grave – the grave of the 'good David', whose life ran from its beginnings in the Old Town to the intellectual salons of France, fame and celebrity, and then back to Scotland to pursue the life of the mind amongst his sometimes less than helpful compatriots. Hume was both an historian and philosopher, but it is for his philosophical scepticism that he is remembered. He was no friend of the theological obfuscation, and proposed a system of understanding the human condition that was based on scrutiny of our impressions and feelings: an unsettling philosophy that seemed to deny a central role to cause and effect. What eighteenth century Scottish philosophy did, through the work of Hume and Smith, was to place feeling and empathy at the forefront of discussions of morality. If sympathy allows us to see the feelings of others, then that will help us to lead a moral life. That line of reasoning has continued to appeal across the centuries and still underpins the work of philosophers who stress the importance of moral imagination. It is not impossible to behave morally if you are devoid of moral imagination – but it is certainly much harder.

The Debating Chamber of the Scottish Parliament
A modern space for modern debates – and, indeed, for good old fashioned arguments. Crafted in oak, sycamore and glass, this chamber is where the Members of the Scottish Parliament conduct their business, watched over from a large public gallery – Scottish Parliament, Licensor Scran

Edinburgh is a realisation, in stone, Scottish philosophical character: spiky

David Hume statue, the Royal Mile, 2014
This wonderful statue is by the Scottish sculptor Alexander Stoddart. Hume never wore a toga, but this is entirely suitable garb for a philosopher who was one of the most influential of his day.
RCAHMS DP194403

The association of Edinburgh with philosophical enquiry is what prompted me to make a philosopher the heroine of one of my Edinburgh series of novels. Isabel Dalhousie is the daughter of a Scottish father and an American mother – her *sainted American mother* as she calls her. She is schooled in Edinburgh, makes a disastrous marriage to a charming but unsuitable Irishman, takes a post-doctoral fellowship in the United States, and then returns to Edinburgh. She lives in the same area in Merchiston that I live in and, like me, has a fox who occasionally inhabits her garden. This is Brother Fox, who lurks under her rhododendrons and pads silently along the top of her walls. He represents nature and unknowable otherness, which is the symbolic literary role of creatures such as foxes and lions, and every so often she sees him staring through her kitchen window with that strange, rather furtive look that foxes give you, as if they see you but do not really want to see you.

Isabel Dalhousie's world proved to be exactly the vehicle that I was looking for in order to write about Edinburgh. I put her in places in the city that I feel have particular resonance: she walks down the atmospheric streets of the Old Town, she meets people in Sandy Bell's pub on the corner of Forrest Road, she has earnest conversations in Candlemaker Row and Queen Street. And all of these places trigger in her mind some philosophical issue – Isabel is given to agonising over things that most of us pass over, and her grappling with these issues leads to her becoming far too involved in events with which she should really

# of a particular sort of
and sceptical

not engage. She cannot help herself, though; if somebody asks for her help, she gives it because the person making the request has entered into a relationship of what she calls *moral proximity* with her.

A few years ago I wrote into one of the Isabel Dalhousie novels a real person whom I had met in New York – Edward Mendelson, the literary executor of W H Auden. I asked Edward whether he minded being given a role in a novel, and when he indicated that he did not, I wrote a scene in which he comes to Edinburgh to deliver a lecture on Auden's work. The following year I was able to translate what happened in the novel into a real event, and arranged for Edward to travel to Edinburgh (in real life) where he delivered – in the magnificent surroundings of the University's Playfair Library – a lecture similar to the one he had delivered in the fictional world of Isabel Dalhousie. We then invited him to go on to dinner in Merchiston, just as he had done in the novel. The other guests at this dinner were all people who had been mentioned in the novels as friends of Isabel Dalhousie, thus bringing together – in real life – people who were connected with one another in the fictional world, where they all had a mutual fictional friend – Isabel Dalhousie.

Edinburgh has always been a city that lends itself to the blurring of the boundaries between what is real and what is not. From Jekyll and Hyde to Jean Brodie, fictional characters are born out of true stories and actual people – but are also the products of the overall atmosphere of the city. In the case of Isabel Dalhousie, the inspiration comes from the intellectual 'feel' of Edinburgh. Yet how does one judge such a thing – if such a concept as intellectual feel even exists? I think that it is quite possible to detect: atmosphere may not be picked up by any scientific instrument, but we know it when we experience it. It is something to do with architecture, perhaps, or setting and architecture, or even *feng shui*, if one believes in such a thing. It is something to do with what we know about a place, about its history and the concerns of the people who live there. It is also something to do, no doubt, with our memories of our own experiences in a place: a place where we have experienced disappointment or rejection may be tainted in our minds and seem forever sad.

I have been in towns where I know there is a history of suffering and violence. I remember visiting many years ago a town in the centre of Sicily that I knew had associations with everything that is wrong with the Italian south: organised crime and oppression. The atmosphere of the place was so uncomfortable, it seemed to me, that I cut short my visit and left within hours of arriving. I have been in a town in the Amazonian jungle that was run, by all accounts, by Colombian drug barons. The villas of these people were there to be seen: opulent, well-defended little castles. The atmosphere was full of foreboding and unspoken threat – or so it seemed to me. This is all very subjective, but it is nonetheless, to me, very real. Detroit smells of industrial defeat and itinerant capitalism; Paris is redolent of light and art; Copenhagen of rationality and civic co-operation. These are all generalisations, of course, but perhaps we need to be able to make them in order to react to our surroundings.

And Edinburgh? I think it is a realisation, in stone, of a particular sort of Scottish philosophical character: spiky and sceptical, but with a strong undercurrent of romance and an appreciation of a certain kind of beauty. It is not a heart-on-sleeve city; it is not an effusive, ebullient city of the sort that a Latin culture may produce; it is, rather, expressive of a Humean sensibility: sympathetic but restrained, articulate but modest in its statements; a city that has no time for the great showy gesture but that can put on a good festival when required; a city that embodies all the bourgeois virtues while also having a rough underbelly. It may not wear its heart on its sleeve, but it certainly has one, tucked away, beating loud and clear when it needs to be heard. It is a city of the mind rather than of the body. It is north rather than south. It is a place that invites you to get to know it, but asks that you don't get too excited in the process. It is a misty dream. It is something that it is not. It is the only place that puts all of this together in this particular way.

The main stair of the Royal Scottish Academy, 1911
This is one of the most charming cultural spaces in the city. A notable feature of the annual offering of the Royal Scottish Academy is an exhibition that allows even unknown artists to display at the heart of Edinburgh's artistic world – a noble and egalitarian tradition.
Francis Caird Inglis, RCAHMS SC466227

The ruins of St Anthony's Chapel, c1830
The links between spirituality and architecture go back to the earliest days of human civilisation. And so it is often the case that – along with fortifications – a city's earliest buildings will likely be related to religion. St Anthony's Chapel, situated on a hillock on the side of Arthur's Seat, is thought to date back to the twelfth century. It may have had close connections to the nearby Holyrood Abbey, built around the same time, and the two buildings were linked by a stone track.
Thomas H Shepherd, RCAHMS DP095285

bottom left and above

Holyrood Abbey, c1850 and c1920

The partial destruction of the Chapel Royal was a mixture of both deliberate action and general neglect. Much was stripped out during the Reformation, and then in the late eighteenth century an attempt at refurbishment went wrong, causing the vault to collapse. The structure has been a ruin ever since, but ruins have their own special appeal. It was here, for instance, that the composer Felix Mendelssohn began his love affair with romantic Scotland: 'Everything is in ruins and mouldering and the bright light of heaven shines in', he remarked of a visit to the Abbey. This was a good thing for Mendelssohn. 'I believe I have found the beginning of my Scottish Symphony there today', he said.

bottom left – T H Flounders, RCAHMS DP096315
above – RCAHMS SCI214569

St Giles' High Kirk, c1880

St Giles' is at the very heart of Edinburgh. Its famous crown spire, although relatively modest in its proportions, is an important landmark, and can be seen from many places across the city. The church was the epicentre of the Protestant Reformation in Scotland, and for a time John Knox was a box-office fixture in its pulpit, guaranteed to say something to inflame passions. Important statements on the social and moral issues of the day are still made here.
Hay and Henderson, RCAHMS SC1105495

St Mary's Episcopal Cathedral, c1900

This Cathedral is of relatively recent construction, having been built at the end of the last century by George Gilbert Scott, a committed gothic-revivalist, who was also responsible for the main building of the University of Glasgow. Associated with a particularly fine choir and music school, St Mary's has, just like St Giles' before it, become a fixture on the Edinburgh skyline. Its three tall and substantial spires act almost like boundary markers to the west end of the New Town.
Alexander Inglis, Scottish Colorfoto,
RCAHMS SC833194

Tolbooth Church, c1910

In Edinburgh one is never far from a church. They have a habit of congregating together – as in my own neighborhood, where one road junction is named 'Holy Corner' because it is overlooked by no less than four churches. Some of these many buildings are still used for worship, while others have been sold on over the years. This is what happened to the Tolbooth Church on Castehill, which is today the Hub festival centre, a venue for numerous artistic events.

Francis Caird Inglis, Scottish Colorfoto, RCAHMS SC1209171

The Tron Kirk, c1920

First built in the late seventeenth century, the Tron Kirk, which lies several hundred yards down the Royal Mile from the Tolbooth, for a time faced an uncertain future. It was closed in the 1950s, and has stood largely empty – and inaccessible to the public – ever since. In recent years, however, it has been enjoying a new lease of life as an entertainment venue during Edinburgh's summer festival season.

Francis Caird Inglis, Scottish Colorfoto, RCAHMS SC436785

St Stephen's Church, 1961

William Playfair's distinctive church building is a wonderfully pleasing sight at the foot of Howe Street. As you walk down the hill from George Street into the residential heart of the New Town, its elegant clock tower frames the view to the Firth of Forth and the hills of Fife beyond. Once again, however, this is no longer a working church. It was put up for sale, and was recently bought by a local philanthropist to be held in trust and managed as a community centre for Stockbridge residents.
RCAHMS SC512087

St Cuthbert's Church and Watchtower, c1915

Sitting in the shadow of the Castle, below the level of Lothian Road, St Cuthbert's is the only church in the foursome here to remain in religious use. A chapel was thought to have been built on this same spot as far back as the ninth century. There is a satisfying continuity to the idea that this one plot of ground, in the centre of the city, has such a long history of spiritual purpose.
Francis M Chrystal, RCAHMS SC1131122

Edinburgh's Parthenon, c1830
Architects often show things in the best possible light and can even make concrete look attractive (on paper). This illustration captures perfectly Edinburgh's ambition to be recognised as the Athens of the North. Here, Calton Hill is crowned by a Scottish Parthenon – an exact replica of the world's most famous ancient building. A public circular – signed by, among others, Walter Scott and Henry Cockburn – explained the reasoning behind the scheme. The Greek Parthenon, it said, 'has stood the test of public admiration for above 2,000 years'. Yet it was also in ruins. It made perfect sense, the circular continued, that it should be rebuilt, and thereby preserved, in Edinburgh, the new intellectual capital of the world. With the 'finest stone quarries' just outside the city, stones could be 'procured at comparatively trifling expense', making it possible to build 'so beautiful an edifice for so very moderate a sum of money'.
Royal Incorporation of Architects in Scotland,
RCAHMS DP103848

Design for a Royal Observatory, Calton Hill, c1817

William Playfair was one of the major architectural influences on the appearance of Edinburgh in the first half of the nineteenth century. It was Playfair – along with the Englishman Charles Robert Cockerell – who was tasked with building the National Monument on Calton Hill. Yet this was just one, albeit the most significant, of a number of buildings intended for the site. The Hill was, and still is, a monument to the ideals of the Enlightenment, and perhaps also to Hubris. This design drawing from 1817 was a young Playfair's grand vision for an Observatory on the site. Note the romantic ruins on the left hand side; the architect would later preside over the construction of the 'ruin' of the National Monument on this very spot. Playfair did build an Observatory on Calton Hill, but to a much simpler and less grand design than the one shown here.

William Henry Playfair, Royal Incorporation of Architects in Scotland, RCAHMS SC756140

**View from the Castle of the
Scottish National Gallery and the
Royal Scottish Academy, c1880**

Edinburgh is fortunate in having great public
buildings at its heart. These two structures
are nothing to do with the commercialism
that can take over a city centre. Instead,
they are symbols of Edinburgh's attitude to
art – an attitude that has made it the home

of numerous cultural festivals throughout
the year. Once again, what we see here
is the work of William Playfair. In these
two photographs from the late nineteenth
century – one looking east, the other looking
west – what stands out is the careful and

deliberate way that the buildings have been
given space to be admired. They were built
to hold works of art, but are also works of
art themselves, and are given pride of place
in the city.

G M Simpson, RCAHMS DP073933

**View of the Scottish National Gallery
and the Royal Scottish Academy from
the Scott Monument, c1870**
RCAHMS SC466228

The Royal Scottish Academy and the Mound from Hanover Street, 1829, 1870 and c1880

The view down Hanover Street to the elegant but authoritative portico of the Royal Scottish Academy is one of the most famous in Edinburgh. Although the building was first built in the 1820s, its adoption of a classical Greek style makes it appear as if has stood on this spot for a great deal longer. In this respect, it is a useful landmark around which we can see the modern city evolve. In the engraving from 1829, there are horses and carriages, and behind the Academy the tall tenements of the Old Town with their reeking lums. By 1870 and 1880, there are two obvious changes. The Assembly Hall on the Mound, with its tall spire, forms the background, and a statue tops the Academy's facade: Queen Victoria recast as Britannia.

Thomas H Shepherd, RCAHMS, DP095281
RCAHMS SC466213
G M Simpson, RCAHMS DP073936

View of the Royal Scottish Academy, 1911, 1961 and 2014

By the twentieth century, motor vehicles have replaced horses and carriages as the major form of traffic passing the Academy. Parked cars line the streets; shop fronts and businesses have come and gone. And increasingly, the portico's columns have become extensions of the exhibitions held within. Every year, they are dressed with colorful imagery and artworks. A familiar view is given a temporary twist. Staid, august tradition meets an overspill of artistic exuberance. It is a glimpse into the beating heart of Edinburgh.

Francis Caird Inglis, RCAHMS SC772077
Eric de Mare, RCAHMS SC466214
RCAHMS DP194397

End

Piece

I like to end each Scotland Street book with a poem.

I write it for one of the principal characters, Angus Lordie, whose affection for the city is expressed at a number of points in the books. This poem comes from *The World According to Bertie*, and we are in Domenica Macdonald's flat in Scotland Street, where Angus and others have been at a dinner party. The poem is about love of place – love of Edinburgh in particular – and about friendship too, and the ties that bind us to our place and to our friends. It is a summer evening, and it is, of course, still light although it is getting late …

Angus put down his cup and moved to the window. There was still a glow of light in the sky, which was high, and empty, the faintest of blues now, washed out. Then he turned round and he saw that every guest, every one present, was a friend, and that he cherished them. So the words came to him and he said:

Dear friends, we are the inhabitants
Of a city which can be loved, as any place may be,
In so many different and particular ways;
But who amongst us can predict
For which reasons, and along which fault lines,
Will the heart of each of us
Be broken? I cannot, for I am moved
By so many different and unexpected things: by our sky,
Which at each moment may change its mood at whim
With clouds in such a hurry to be somewhere else;
By our lingering haars, by our eccentric skyline,
All crags and spires and angular promises,
By the way we feel in Scotland, yes, simply that;
These are the things that break my heart
In a way for which I am never quite prepared –
The surprises of a love affair that lasts a lifetime.
But what breaks the heart the most, I think,
Is the knowledge that what we have
We all must lose; I don't much care for denial,
But if pressed to say goodbye, that final word
On which even the strongest can stumble,
I am not above pretending
That the party continues elsewhere,
With a guest list that is mostly the same,
And every bit as satisfactory;
That what we think are ends are really adjournments,
An entr'acte, an interval, not real goodbyes;
And perhaps they are, dear friends, perhaps they are.

Fishmarket Close, c1940
H D Wylie, RCAHMS SC801614

Acknowledgements

The research that underpins this book was prepared for the exhibition *A Tale of Two Cities*. Thanks are due to Kirsty Devine of Making Stories, Tim Pethick of Nomad Exhibitions and the team at Nanjing Museum, China. The preparation of this volume has benefited from the input of many staff within RCAHMS. These include Robert Adam, Rebecca Bailey, Zoe Ballantine, Oliver Brookes, Alasdair Burns, James Crawford, Tahra Duncan-Clark, Lesley Ferguson, Simon Green, Anne Martin, Derek Smart, Steve Wallace and Kristina Watson. Thanks are also due to Jan Rutherford, Linda Sutherland, Mairi Sutherland and Agnieszka Urbanska.

Royal Commission on the Ancient and Historical Monuments of Scotland

List of Commissioners

Index

Abbotsford bar 63, *64*
Adam, Robert 25, *42, 44,* 91, *115*
　see also Old College
Adam, William *86, 176*
Aikenhead, Thomas 194
Alexander, Christopher 14
Allen, J & R 125
Anchor Close 61
Anchor Tavern 61
architecture 125, 126, 201
　churches 196
　Edinburgh University 56, 91, 92
　New Town 12, 23, 25, 87
　Old Town 16, 17, 19, 20
　Princes Street *144*
　schools 83, 84, 87, 88, *103*
Arthur's Seat *30, 33, 72,* 171, *183, 184, 204*
Assembly Hall *195, 218*
Atholl Crescent, domestic science college 11, 94
Auden, W H 125, 201

Baillie, Matthew 168
Ballantyne, James, and Co 133
Balmoral Hotel 126
　see also North British Hotel
'Banana Flats', Leith *68*
Bank of Scotland 131, *131,* 154
Barker, Pat 170
Bartholomew, John 135
Batty, Lt-Col *183*
Baxter's Close *59*
Beehive Hotel *138*
Belgrave Crescent Gardens *15*
Bell, Benjamin 168
Bell, Joseph 168
Bell, Sandy, Sandy Bell's bar 63, 200
Bell Wig Maker and Hair Cutter *141*
Birlinn 135
Blackfriars Street 84, 133
Bristo Place 92
British Linen Bank 131, *157*
Brodie, Deacon 61
Brown, George Mackay *64*
Brunsfield Place 132
Bruntsfield Primary School *103*
Bryce, David *157, 167, 178,* 180
Bryson, Bill 56
Buccleuch Place 56
Buchan, James 91
Buchanan, George 56, 58, *72*
Burke and Hare 9, 168, *175*
Burns, Robert 23, 26, 56, 196
　in Edinburgh 9, 20, 59, *60,* 61, *71*
　Fergusson's influence 20, 58–9, *59*

monument *72, 97*
Butlin, Ron 66

Cables Wynd *68*
Café Royal 63, *64*
Calton Hill 23, *193,* 196, 199, *215*
　see also National Monument; Royal High School
Calton Road *9*
Cameron, Lord (Jock Cameron) *53*
Canal Street Station 127
Candlemaker Row *78, 79,* 200
Canongate 20, *109,* 161
Canongate Kirk 17, 20, 196, *197*
Canongate Kirkyard 20, 58–9, *59, 99*
Canongate Press 133
Canonmills 127
Captains Bar 9, 11
Carlyle, Thomas 56, 133
Carnegie, Andrew 22
Castle Rock see Edinburgh Castle
Castle Terrace 17
Causewayside, Southern Motors Filling Station *136*
Chambers Street *39,* 91, 94, 125, *189*
　see also National Museum of Scotland
Charlotte Square 25, *42, 47, 50,* 135
children's games 83–4
Church of Scotland 193–4, *195*
churches/religion 17, 193–6
Cockburn, Henry 121, *138,* 213
Cockburn Street *38, 163*
Cockerell, Charles *199, 215*
Colinton 169
Colinton Road *84,* 94
College Street 9, 58
Constable, T & A 133
Contini, Philip and Mary 122
Cowgate 9, *38, 39, 78,* 168
Craig House 169
Craig, James 23
Craigleith Quarry *33*
Craiglockhart House 170
Crofton, Sir John 169
Cronin, A J 170
Cullen, William 168
Cumberland Street 12, 26
Cunninghame, Tom *78, 105, 144*
Currie, Dr Colin 169
Curryhill House 166

Dalry 132
Daniel Stewart's School/College 87, *103*
Darnley, Henry *9, 76*
David I, King of Scots 16
David Hume Tower *119*
Davie, George 62
Deacon Brodie tavern 61
Dean Bridge 11, *161,* 169
Dean Village 11, *83, 161*
Demarco, Richard 125
Dickens, Charles 55
Dickson's Close 166
Dominion Cinema 169
Donizetti, Gaetano 55
Doric Tavern *134,* 136
Dough School, Atholl Crescent 11, 94
Dovecot Tapestry Studios 84
Doyle, Arthur Conan 169
Drummond, James *59*
Drummond Place 26
Dunbar, William 56
Duncan, Dr 166
Duncan's Land 11
Dundas Street 26, 122, 172
Dunn and Findlay *153*

Easter Road 132
Edinburgh, Duke of 23
Edinburgh Academy 88–9
'Edinburgh at Night' 78
Edinburgh Castle 15, 17, 122, *183, 184*
　Grassmarket and *35, 38, 123*
　Lawnmarket and *26*
　'Prospect of Edinburgh from the North' *30*
　Scottish National Gallery and Royal Academy from *216*
　trams against *121*
Edinburgh Merchant Company schools 88, *105, 106–7*
Edinburgh Napier University 12, 94, *94,* 170
Edinburgh Public Library 20, 22
Edinburgh Royal Infirmary *165,* 166, 169, *176–81*
Edinburgh Savings Bank, Hanover Street *154*
Edinburgh Underground *128,* 129–30
Edinburgh University 9, 84, 89, 91–2, 94
　architecture 56, 91, 92
　George Square library *91, 113*
　Medical School 92, *116, 174*
　Men's Union 11
　Pollock Halls of Residence 89
　　see also McEwan Hall; Old College; Playfair Library
Edinburgh University Press 94, 135
education 82–119
　see also Edinburgh Napier University; Edinburgh University; Heriot-Watt University; Queen Margaret University
Edwards, Owen Dudley 136
Elgin, Earl of 199
Enlightenment 20, 25, 129, 168, 193, *215*

Ferguson, Adam 20
Fergusson, Robert 20, 58–9, *59*
Fettes College 88, *103*
Fiddes, Dr F S 92
Fish Market 121
　see also Fruit, Vegetable and Fish Market
Fishmarket Close *221*
　see also Old Fishmarket Close
Fleming, Ian 88
Fleshmarket 121
Flodden Tower *109*
Forest Row 200
　see also Sandy Bell's bar
Forsyth, R & W 125
Fountainbridge 132
Frederick Street *121, 143, 146*
Fruit, Vegetable and Fish Market *138*

Garioch, Robert 26, 58–9, 63, *64,* 126, *152*
General Assembly 193–4, *195*
George Heriot's School/Hospital *37, 72, 86,* 87, 88, *100, 176*
George IV Bridge 17, 20, *78*
George Square 56, 91, 92, *113, 118, 119,* 135
George Street 23, 25, *46–7,* 132, *159,* 168
George Watson's School/College *84,* 87, *103*
Gillespie, James, School/Hospital 89, 103
Gladstone's Land *71*
Glass and Thompson's bistro 122
Goldberg's building 125
Gordon, Duchess of *60*

Gordon of Rothiemay's bird's eye view *28*
Granton Harbour railway line 127, 129
Grassmarket 17, *35, 38, 78,* 121, *123, 138*
Graves, Robert 170
Gray, James, and Son *159*
Greyfriars Kirk 17
Greyfriars Kirkyard 56, 58, *72, 184*
Grieve, Christopher M (Hugh MacDiarmid) 23, 63, *64*
Guthrie Street *39*

Hanover Street *154, 218*
Haymarket Station 127
Henderson, Hamish 63, 65
Heriot, George *37, 72, 86,* 87, 88, *100, 176*
Heriot Row 25, *50,* 61, 172
Heriot-Watt University 94
Higgs, Peter 170, 171–2, *171*
High Kirk see St Giles' High Kirk / Cathedral
High School see Royal High School
High Street 16, *16,* 17, *36,* 61, 129, 131, 133
　see also Canongate Kirk; Parliament Square; Royal Mile
Hodge, Robin 133
Hogg, James 133
Holy Corner 94, *210*
Holy Trinity Church *15*
Holyrood 15, 135, *184,* 193
Holyrood Abbey 17, *204,* 205
Holyrood Park 171
Holyroodhouse/Holyrood Palace *16,* 20, *30, 159,* 194
Horner, Francis 56
Howe Street *211*
Hume, David 20, 23, 25, 130, 199, *200,* 202
　David Hume Tower *119*
Hunter, John 168
Hutton, James 20, 170–1, *170,* 172, *183, 184*

Incorporation of Surgeons and Barbers of Edinburgh 166
India Place *108*
industry 130, 132–3, *158–9*
Infirmary Street 84, *176–7*

Jamaica Place 25–6
James IV, King of Scots 165–6
James VI, King of Scots *36,* 58, *76,* 89, 91
James Ballantyne and Co 133
James Gillespie's School/Hospital 89, *103*
James Gray and Son *159*
James Soutar's shop *141*
Jeffrey Street 133
Jenner's 125, *125, 144,* 146

Kay, James 20, 194
Kay, John 65
Keith, Dr 166
Kelly, Stewart 55
Kemp, George Meikle *75*
King's Stables Road 17
Kirk o'Fields 9, 91
Knox, John *117,* 194, *195, 207*
Knox, Dr Robert 168

Lady Lawson Street 125
Lady Stair's Close *59, 80*
Lady Stair's House *71*
Lansdowne Crescent, Peddie's house *45*
Lauder, Harry 55

Lauriston Place *84, 165, 176, 178*
Lawnmarket *18, 20, 26*, 61, *141*
Leith 66, 68, 183
    see also Water of Leith
Leith Walk 122
Lennox, Duke of 58
Lindsay Stewart Lecture Theatre *94*
literature 20, 26, 54–81, 200–1
Lochhead, Liz 56
Lorimer, Hugh *20*
Lothian Road *74, 150–1*
Lownie, Andrew 61
Luckenbooths, the 133
Lyndsey, David 56

MacCaig, Norman 63, *64*
MacDiarmid, Hugh (Christopher M
    Grieve) 23, 63, *64*
McEwan Hall 11, *117*
McGonagall, William Topaz 56, 58, *72*
McGuffie, Mr 136
McIntosh, Iain *128*
McKay, Lucinda *172*
McKean, Charles *100*
McKellar, Kenneth 55
Mackenzie, Compton 26
MacKenzie, Sir George *72*
Maclean, Sorley 63, *64*
maps/plans
    Edinburgh *35*
    New Town *24, 35, 40*
    Old Town *28, 31, 35, 183*
    poem about *12*
    see also Gordon of Rothiemay's
        bird's eye view
Marchmont, bell pulls *10*
Marcus Furs, Frederick Street *143*
Market Street 135, *163*
markets 17, 121–2
    see also Fish Market; Fleshmarket;
        Fruit, Vegetable and Fish Market;
        Grassmarket; Lawnmarket;
        Waverley Market
Martyrs' Monument *72*
Mary Erskine School *103*
Mary, Queen of Scots *76*
Massie, Allan 25
Maxwell, James Clerk 23, 88
Meadows, the *84, 92, 169, 178*
Medical School, Edinburgh University
    92, 116, 174
medicine 164–70
Mendelson, Cheryl 26
Mendelson, Edward 201
Mendelssohn, Felix 55, *205*
Mercat Cross 20, *36*, 129, 172
Merchiston 200, 201
Milne's Bar 63, *64*
Moffat, Alexander 63, *64*
Molière 56
Monro, Alexander *175*
Monro family 168
Moray Place 25, 26, *53*
Morgan, Edwin *64*
Morningside 62, 135, 169
Mound, the 23, *154*, 193, 218

Napier, Sir John 94
Napier University 12, 94, *94*, 170
National Gallery of Scotland 127, 130,
    148, 216–17
    see also Scottish National Portrait
        Gallery
National Library of Scotland 20, *20*, 22
National Monument 99, 196, 199, *213,
    214, 215*
National Museum of Scotland *39*, 94,
    189–90

Nelson Street 26
Nelson, Thomas 133
New Club 129, *147*
New College *115*, 193
New Street Gasworks *161*
New Town 15, 23–6, *33, 40–1,*
    135, 196
    architecture 12, 23, 25, 87
    construction 20, 23, *33*
    maps/plans *24, 35, 40*
Newcraighall 94
Newington 135
Nicolson Street see Surgeon's Hall
Nightingale, Florence *180*
Nor Loch 23
North Bridge 23, *138, 163*
    see also Scotsman building
North British Hotel 126, *127, 144,
    152–3*
North British Rubber Company 132

Old College 9, *39*, 91, *92, 115*
    see also Playfair Library
Old Fishmarket Close 121
    see also Fishmarket Close
Old Playhouse Close, James Soutar's
    shop *141*
Old Town 11, 15–23, *33*, 56, *141, 184,*
    218
    in McCall Smith's novels 200
    maps/plans *28, 31, 35, 183*
    markets 121
Oliver and Boyd 133
Opie, Iona and Peter 84
Owen, Wilfred 170
Oxford Bar *62*, 63

Palace of Holyroodhouse see
    Holyroodhouse/Holyrood Palace
Panmure House 20
Parliament House 193
Parliament Square 22, 61
Peddie, James, house *45*
Peploe, Guy *64*, 122
Peploe, Samuel 122
Pevsner, Sir Nicholas *214*
Physicians' Hall 168
plans see maps/plans
Playfair Library 9, 22, *91, 113*, 201
Playfair, William
    National Monument 196, 199
    Royal Observatory *215*
    St Stephen's Church 88, *211*
    Scott Monument competition entry
        74
    Scottish National Gallery and Royal
        Scottish Academy *216*
    Surgeon's Hall 166, *175*
Plaza Ballroom 135
Pleasance, the *171*
'Poets' Pub' 63, *64*
Pollock Halls of Residence 89
Princes Mall 121
Princes Street 23, 55, 125, 126, *146–7*
    Edinburgh Castle from *184*
    Edinburgh Underground 129
    from Cockburn Street *38*
    old trams *121*
    St John's Church *74*
    see also North British Hotel
Princes Street Gardens *12*, 80, *109,
    143, 148, 183*
Princes Street Railway Station *150–1*
'Prospect of Edinburgh from the North'
    30–1

Queen Margaret University 94
Queen Street 44, *103*, 166, 168, 200

Raeburn, Sir Henry 91, *170*, 172
Ramsay, Allan 56, *72*, 133
Ramsay Garden *143*, 193
Ramsay Lane *184*
Rankin, Ian 63, 66, *69*
Regent Road 72, 84
Reinhard, Robert *69*
religion 17, 193–6
Riddle's Court 20
Rivers, William 170
Roget, Dr Peter M 135
Royal Bank of Scotland, St Andrews
    Square 154
Royal College of Physicians *44*, 166,
    167, 168
Royal College of Surgeons 166, 168
    see also Surgeon's Hall
Royal Edinburgh Hospital 169
Royal High School 84, 92, *96–9*, 193
Royal Infirmary see Edinburgh Royal
    Infirmary
Royal Mile *71, 141, 200*
    see also Bank of Scotland;
        Canongate; High Street
Royal Observatory *215*
Royal Scottish Academy *109, 130,
    202, 216–19*
Royal Society of Edinburgh 23, 171

St Andrew's and St George's Church
    46
St Andrew's Square 25, *46*, 129, 130,
    154, 157
St Anthony's Chapel *33, 204*
St Cuthbert's Church *211*
St David's Street *146*
St George's Church *33, 47*
St Giles' High Kirk/Cathedral 17, *18,
    22, 26, 30*, 61, 194, *207*
St James Centre 125
St John's Church *74*
St John's Close *109*
St John's Hill 171
St Leonard's (mansion) 89
St Mary's Cathedral 125, *207*
St Stephen's Church 88, *211*
St Stephen's Street 11
St Trinean's school 89
St Vincent Street 88
Salisbury Crags *72*, 171, *183, 184*
Samson's Ribs *183*
Sandy Bell's bar 63, 200
Sassoon, Siegfried 170
schools 82–9, *103*
    see also Dough School; Edinburgh
        Merchant Company schools;
        George Heriot's School/Hospital;
        Royal High School
science and medicine 164–91
Scotland Street *26*, 66
Scotland Street tunnel *66*, 127, 129
'Scotland's Industrial Souvenir' *158–9*
Scotsman building 121, 125, 135, *163*
Scott, George Gilbert *207*
Scott, Sir Walter 9, 20, *36*, 55, 56,
    88, *213*
    monument 23, 55, *55, 56, 74–7,
        217*
Scottish Enlightenment 20, 25, 129,
    168, 193, *215*
Scottish Gallery 122
Scottish National Gallery see National
    Gallery of Scotland
Scottish National Portrait Gallery 23,
    63, *64*, 172
Scottish Parliament *16*, 193, *193*, 199
Scottish Vulcanite Company 132
Searle, Ronald 89

Serlio, Sebastiano 87
shopping 121–2
Signet Library 22–3, 61
Simpson, Dr James Young 166
Simpson Memorial Pavilion 169
Slezer, John *30, 100*
Smellie, William 61, 168
Smith, Adam 20, 130, 199
Smith, Henry *76*
Smith, Iain Crichton *64*
Smith, Sir Sidney 92
Smith, Sydney 56
Smith, Sydney Goodsir 26, 63, *64*
Soutar, James, shop *141*
South Bridge see Bank of Scotland; Old
    College
Southern Motors Filling Station *136*
Spark, Muriel 65, 89
Spence, Sir Basil *113*
Stevenson, Robert Louis 9, 20, *50,*
    61, *65*
Stewart, Daniel, School/College 87,
    103
Stockbridge 11, 26, *108*
Stoddart, Alexander 23, *200*
Stuart, Esmé (Duke of Lennox) 58
Surgeon's Hall 166, *172, 175*
    see also Royal College of Surgeons

Talbot Rice Gallery *91*
Teviot Place see McEwan Hall
Thistle Street 63, 133
Thompson, Patrick 125
Tolbooth Church *210*
Tollcross 125
trade and commerce 130–6
    see also markets; shopping
Traquair, Phoebe Anna 129
Tron Kirk *30*, 121, 210
Tron Square *39*
Tweeddale Court 133
Tynecastle 132

Union Palais dance hall 11
universities see Edinburgh University;
    Heriot-Watt University; Napier
    University; Queen Margaret
    University

Valvona and Crolla 122
Vennel, the *109, 184*
Victoria, Queen 58, 218
Victoria Street 17, *37*, 122

Wallace, William (master mason) 87
Warriston Cemetery *69*
Water of Leith 11, *35*, 132, 169
    see also Dean Bridge; Dean Village
Waterloo Place *9*
Watson, George, School/College *84,*
    87, 103
Waugh, Evelyn 88
Waverley Bridge *38*
Waverley Market 121
Waverley Station 121, 126, 127, 129,
    138, 148, 153
Welsh, Irvine *66, 68*
West Port 168
West Register House *47*
Wolfe-Murray, Stephanie 133
Wood, Wendy 92
working lives 120–63
Writers' Museum *59, 71*

Zyw, Alexander 11